SPELLING RULES!

Second edition

Helen Pearson
and Janelle Ho

STUDENT BOOK 6

Makes Spelling stick!

Name: ______________________________

Class: ______________________________

macmillan education

Contents

SLLURP

SLLURP summarises the spelling strategies that you can use to learn new words.

Say	Say the word carefully and slowly to yourself.
Listen	Listen to how each part of the word sounds in sequence.
Look	Look at the patterns of letters in the word and the shape of the word.
Understand	Understand rules, word meanings and word origins.
Remember	Remember all the similar words you can already spell and relate this knowledge to any new word.
Practise	Practise writing the word until it is firmly fixed in your long-term memory.

Scope and Sequence

This scope and sequence chart is based on the requirements of the Australian Curriculum.

Unit	Page	Skill focus					
		Sound-letter patterns	Prefixes and suffixes (morphology)	Other morphology	Etymology	Homophones/ Homographs/ Confusing words	Topic words
1	6	ge, gi, gy, dge, j					
2	8		-ion: adding to t, nt, lve				
3	10		-ion: adding to silent e, de				
4	12	words ending in a vowel sound					
5	14		suffixes	abbreviations		premier, cabinet, minister	government
6	16	REVISION					
7	18	er, ir, or, ur, ear, our					
8	20		-er, -or, -ian, -ist				occupations
9	22		-ity: adding to ible, able				
10	24					confusing pairs	
11	26		affixes; -logy				environment
12	28	REVISION					
13	30	ion, ior, ian, iar	-ity				
14	32	al, el, le	-al			serial/cereal, metal/mettle	
15	34		-ous				
16	36				nova, vox, notare, reminisci	novel	
17	38		-ic	word elements scope, meter			science
18	40	REVISION					
19	42		-ion, -ation, -ition	abbreviations			
20	44	ary, ery, ory				salary/celery, summary/summery	
21	46			word elements mono, multi, omni, poly			
22	48				phone, onyma, patheia, magnus		
23	50			abbreviations		organ, appendix	medicine
24	52	REVISION					
25	54	cy	-cy, ob-				
26	56	double consonants					
27	58	cc					
28	60		adding multiple affixes				
29	62		suffixes; plurals		non-English words		money
30	64	REVISION					
31	66	sce, sci					
32	68			odd-looking words			
33	70				non-English words		
34	72			idioms	astro		space and time
35	74	REVISION OF UNITS 1–34					

Note to teachers and parents

Some students are natural spellers. But the vast majority of students need formal, systematic and sequential instruction about the way spelling works and the strategies they can use to become independent, confident spellers and spelling risk-takers.

The *Spelling Rules!* program is based on sound linguistic and pedagogical theory. It is informed by research into how students of different ages acquire and apply spelling skills, and how those skills move from the working to the long-term memory. The program closely follows the Australian English curriculum. *Australian Curriculum: English* references are provided in the Teacher Resource Books. The program consists of seven Student Books, fully supported by two Teacher Resource Books.

Each student book contains units of work, with each unit designed to be used over the course of a week. The content of each unit simultaneously develops new skills and reinforces skills from previous units and earlier books. The introduction of new letter patterns is logically sequenced and takes into account both frequency of use and complexity. Where appropriate, topic words from other curriculum areas such as mathematics, science and social sciences are included. When spelling rules are introduced, only known sounds and letter patterns are used so that students focus on one skill at a time. Regular revision units enable teachers to assess student progress and reinforce key rules and patterns from previous units.

Spelling knowledge

Learning to spell involves developing different kinds of spelling knowledge. In many cases, particularly in the upper grades, more than one kind of knowledge is called upon at a time. As they work through the activities in each *Spelling Rules!* unit, students will develop:

- ☆ **Kinaesthetic knowledge** – the physical feeling when saying different sounds and words, and when writing the shapes of letters and words
- ☆ **Phonological knowledge** – how a word sounds and the patterns of sounds in words
- ☆ **Visual knowledge** – how letters and words look and the visual patterns in words
- ☆ **Morphemic knowledge** – the meaning or function of words or parts of words
- ☆ **Etymological knowledge** – the origins and history of words and the effect this has on spelling patterns.

Icons used in Student Book 6

Rule! This icon highlights useful spelling rules. The rule is always introduced the first time students will need it to complete an activity. There is also a handy summary of important rules on page 80.

Tip! This icon tells students that a special clue or hint is provided for an activity. It may be a spelling, grammar or punctuation convention, or a definition of a useful term.

Student Book 6

Units of work

Student Book 6 contains 35 weekly units of work. See the **Scope and Sequence chart** on page 3 for more information.

Word lists

Spelling lists enable a particular rule, letter pattern, sound pattern, etymology or morphemic element to be focused on and they provide sufficient examples to consolidate the teaching point.
In *Student Book 6*, each unit (except Revision) has a list of fifteen spelling words. The core words in the lists have been chosen to support the learning focus and strategies being taught in the unit. Topic words come from other curriculum areas, such as mathematics and social sciences. In addition, homophones and words that are easily confused with each other are explained and practised.

The lists also include words to challenge the best spellers and provide the platform for teachers to extend their students' spelling ability and vocabulary.

SLLURP

Each word list begins with a reminder for students to SLLURP. SLLURP summarises the strategies that will help spelling move from students' working memory to their long-term memory. These strategies are provided on page 2, for easy reference.

Unit at a glance

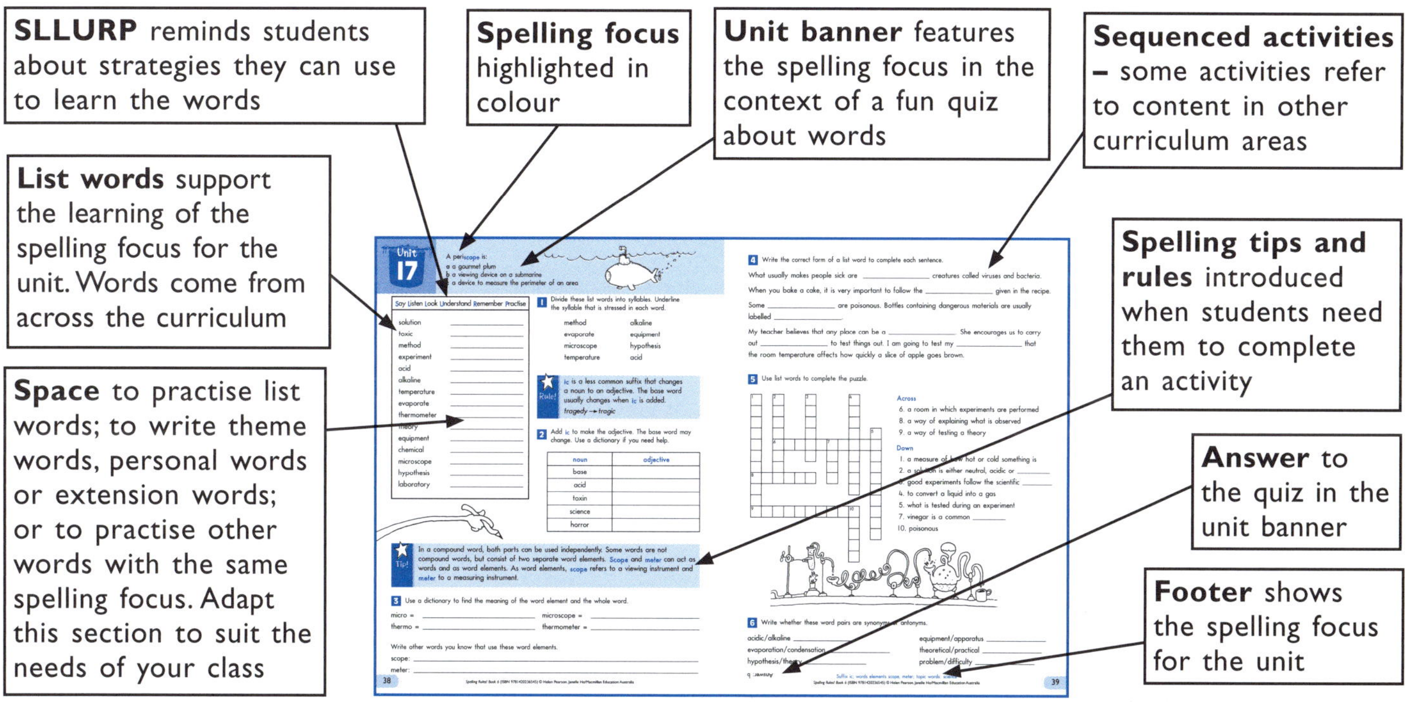

Spelling Rules! Teacher Resource Book 3–6

Full teacher support for *Student Book 6* is provided by *Spelling Rules! Teacher Resource Book 3-6*. Here you will find valuable background information about spelling development and spelling knowledge, along with practical resources, such as:

- ☆ teaching tips for every unit in *Student Book 6*
- ☆ extra word lists
- ☆ strategies for teaching spelling
- ☆ guidelines for assessment and diagnosis of errors
- ☆ activities to support struggling spellers
- ☆ worthwhile extension for more able spellers.

Unit 1

Julienne describes:

a the naming of a baby girl
b something cut into thin strips
c plans for a party in July

Say Listen Look Understand Remember Practise

average	________
advantage	________
passenger	________
urgent	________
fragile	________
revenge	________
challenge	________
pledge	________
justice	________
rejoice	________
junction	________
prejudice	________
adjacent	________
adjustment	________
judgement	________

Tip! G usually has a soft sound when it is followed by **e**, **i** or **y**.

1 Circle the letter **g** if it has a soft sound.

gentle	energy	goalpost
gigantic	garden	gymnasium
genius	ginger	gear
golden	giddy	general

2 Use some of the letters in each word to make new words with a hard **g** sound.

passenger ________
urgent ________
challenge ________
pledge ________
average ________

Tip! Prefixes and suffixes are known as **affixes**.

3 Break each word into its base word and affix.

urgently = ________ + ________
judgement = ________ + ________
adjustment = ________ + ________
disadvantage = ________ + ________

4 Use the list words as verbs, nouns and adjectives. Try not to use the same word more than once.

verbs	nouns	adjectives
to ________ in a win	an immediate ________	an ________ request
to ________ one team	a minor ________	a ________ model
to ________ loyalty	to seek ________	of ________ weight
to ________ yourself	a complicated ________	two ________ buildings

5 Write list words belonging to the same word family. Use a dictionary if you need help.

vengeful joy judge

_______________ _______________ _______________ _______________ _______________

6 Complete the passage.

In the Australian _______________ system, anybody accused of a crime is defended by a lawyer. In court, there is a _______________, who knows the law and controls what happens in the courtroom. A group of ordinary people called the _______________ makes the final decision about whether the defendant is guilty. If not guilty, the accused is free to leave. If guilty, the judge makes a _______________ about an appropriate punishment.

7 Write list words.

The contents of the box are _______________. Please carry it carefully.

We live _______________ to a park, so I play there with my sister every day.

Mum made an _______________ to the length of my pyjamas so my little brother could wear them.

In a game, the home team usually has an _______________.

A judge must always act fairly if the accused is to receive _______________.

I am of _______________ height, but my sister is tall for her age.

Karl longed to travel as a _______________ on the Trans-Siberian railway.

My father has a _______________ against cats, because they make him sneeze.

8 Describe an amazing journey using as many list words as you can. Try to include other words with a soft g sound.

____

____

____

____

____

____

____

____

____

____

Answer: b

Unit 2

What does pretension mean?

a a claim that you deserve merit when you don't
b a number before ten
c preparing tent ropes

Say Listen Look Understand Remember Practise	
rejection	______
detection	______
exhibition	______
exhaustion	______
digestion	______
distinction	______
admission	______
permission	______
submission	______
extension	______
suspension	______
expansion	______
evolution	______
resolution	______
revolution	______

1 Write the two list words that have a silent letter.

______ ______

2 Complete the table.

verb	noun
attract	
	injection
	detection
exhibit	
exhaust	
	digestion
reject	
	direction
	infection
inspect	

Rule!

For some words ending in **t**, change **t** to **ss** before adding **ion**.
admit → admission

If a word ends in **nd**, change **d** to **s** before adding **ion**.
extend → extension

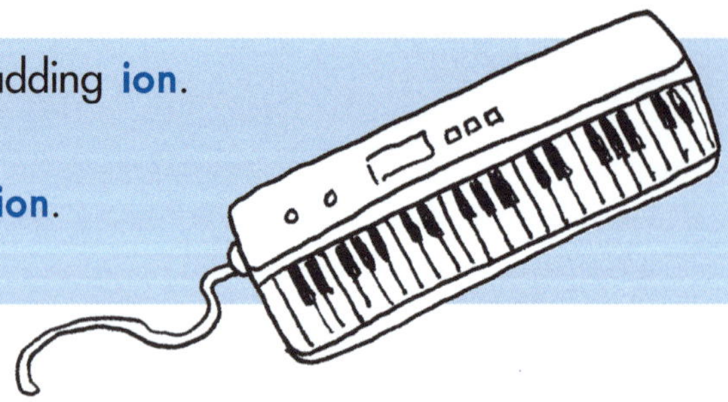

3 Write the noun.

permit ______ submit ______ omit ______
expand ______ suspend ______ comprehend ______

4 *Admit* has two related nouns: *admission* and *admittance*. Use a dictionary to find the meaning of each word. Use each word in a sentence.

admission: ______

______

admittance: ______

______

Spelling Rules! Book 6 (ISBN 9781420236545) © Helen Pearson, Janelle Ho/Macmillan Education Australia

Rule! If a word ends in **lve**, change **ve** to **ut** before adding **ion**.
dissolve → dissolution

5 Make a noun by adding **ion**.

evolve ________ resolve ________ solve ________ revolve ________

6 Use the clue to make a new word that matches the definition.

word	clue	new word	definition
detection	change a letter	________	gloominess
distinction	change 1st syllable	________	end of a species
digestion	change 1st syllable	________	build-up of traffic
revolution	change a letter	________	conclusion

7 Rewrite each sentence using a list word. If you can, begin your sentence with the list word.

The scientist Charles Darwin proposed a theory of how living things have evolved.

____

This year I have resolved to talk to one new person a month.

____

The local council has finally said they will permit my parents to build a pool!

____

My prize-winning painting will be exhibited in the Town Hall next month.

____

Anyone caught writing graffiti on the walls will be suspended.

____

8 Proofread this text. The text has six words that are incorrect. Circle the mistakes. Then write the correct spelling of the words in the boxes.

I knew the little cakes on the bench were for morning tea and I would never get permition to have one now. Maybe the solussion was to sneak a couple while no one was around, and avoid detecsion. I had one in my hand when Dad came into the kitchen, so I stuffed it in my mouth. Eating that quickly is bad for the digeston! I've made a resolusion not to do it again, as it's better than making an admition with your mouth full!

Answer: a

Spelling Rules! Book 6 (ISBN 9781420236545) © Helen Pearson, Janelle Ho/Macmillan Education Australia

Unit 3

Fluctuation occurs when:

a fruit becomes rotten
b a flock of ducks flies in formation
c something changes constantly

Say Listen Look Understand Remember Practise

desperation	______
cooperation	______
appreciation	______
devastation	______
association	______
deception	______
prescription	______
explosion	______
decision	______
erosion	______
invasion	______
exclusion	______
collision	______
persuasion	______
provision	______

Rule! Some verbs add **ion** to make the noun. If the verb ends in silent **e**, drop the **e** before adding **ion**.
devote → devotion

1 Write the noun form.

impress	separate
______	______
pollute	cooperate
______	______

2 Write the base word.

education	irrigation
______	______
discussion	desperation
______	______
appreciation	devastation
______	______

Rule! If the verb ends in **de**, drop the **e** and change **d** to **s** before adding **ion**.
divide → division

3 Write the noun form.

explode	collide	invade	exclude	persuade
______	______	______	______	______
conclude	include	erode	decide	evade
______	______	______	______	______

4 Change these verbs to nouns using the same pattern. Describe the pattern.

discuss → ______ ______
possess → ______ ______
obsess → ______ ______

Tip! Some words are always used together. This is called **collocation**.
separation from not *separation with*
The underlined words are **prepositions**.

5 Write a list word and the preposition it goes with to complete each sentence.

The player's ________________ ________ the first team was due to injury.

The ________________ ________ the riverbank resulted in deep gullies.

To show our ________________ ________ our grandmother, we bought her some flowers.

The shattered glass at the intersection was due to the ________________ ________ two cars earlier.

Our school fete was a success due to ________________ ________ the parents and the local community.

Mum has had a long ________________ ________ the Red Cross.

6 Complete the table. All the words follow the same pattern.

verb	noun
describe	descri**ption**
prescribe	
subscribe	
inscribe	
transcribe	

7 Complete the table. All the words follow the same pattern.

verb	noun
dec**eive**	
	perception
	conception
receive	

Answer: c

Unit 4

What is whang**ee**?

a the opposite of a wedgie
b bamboo used for making canes
c someone who has made one hundred bungee jumps

Say Listen Look Understand Remember Practise	
flee	
pursue	
statue	
venue	
cocoa	
mosquito	
rodeo	
eerie	
simile	
guarantee	
refugee	
committee	
verandah	
debut	
alibi	

1 Write list words that end with these sounds.

long o as in toe

long e as in key

long oo as in true

2 Write a list word that has a silent letter.

3 Which list word is a homophone? Write each word and its meaning.

4 Write the plural.

verandah mosquito refugee volcano alibi

5 Write the language each word comes from, and its meaning. Use a dictionary if you need help.

	language	meaning
cocoa		
rodeo		
verandah		
debut		
alibi		

6 Most of the vowels have been left out of these sentences. Write each sentence correctly.

Ths nw cmptr gdgt cms wth a fr-yr grnte.

____

Th wnd whstlng thrgh th crck in th wndw mks n eri snd.

____

Do y knw th vnu fr th drss rhrsl?

____

Lins prsu thr pry in pcks t incrs thr chncs of mkng a kll.

____

Tip!

A **simile** describes something by comparing it to something else.
It uses *like* or *as* to make the comparison.
The dancer flopped around like a fish out of water.
The dancer moved as gracefully as a swan.

7 Write similes using these words.

statue: ______________________________

cocoa: ______________________________

eerie: ______________________________

rodeo: ______________________________

mosquito: ______________________________

8 Write list words.

The local community hall will be a good ____________ for our meeting.

Hot____________ can warm you up in winter.

The ____________ net around my bed has a hole in it, and I got bitten last night.

The light before the thunderstorm was ____________.

9 Write the correct form of the verb to complete each sentence.

The police ____________ the shoplifters and eventually caught them.
pursue

This gold pass ____________ you free entry to the movies for one year!
guarantee

Our cat Mimi ____________ into the house when the dogs started barking.
flee

Answer: b

Unit 5

A diarchy is:

a two arches in a row
b a human with two heads
c a State governed by two rulers

Say Listen Look Understand Remember Practise

government ______
parliament ______
cabinet ______
politician ______
minister ______
senator ______
representatives ______
governor ______
premier ______
opposition ______
president ______
election ______
democracy ______
monarchy ______
federal ______

1 Break each word into its base word and suffix.

government = ______ + ______
election = ______ + ______
monarchy = ______ + ______
opposition = ______ + ______
politician = ______ + ______
president = ______ + ______
governor = ______ + ______

2 Look at the words in question 1.

Which words have the same base word?

______ ______

In which words does the base word change when the suffix is added?

______ ______ ______

3 Write the list words that refer to people who work in government. Circle the word that is not a head of Australian government.

______ ______ ______ ______
______ ______ ______

4 Many abbreviations are used in government. What do these abbreviations stand for?

PM ______ MHR ______
MP ______ GG ______

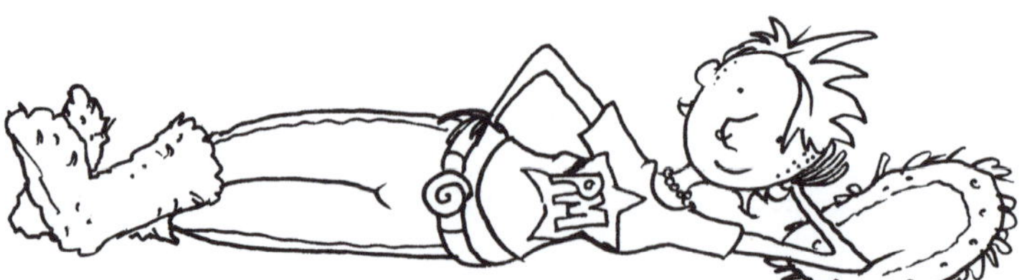

5 Write commonly used abbreviations for these words.

federal ______ government ______ representatives ______

6 Look up each word in a dictionary. Write a definition and the language each one comes from.

monarchy ______________________________

____

democracy ______________________________

____

> **Tip!** A word that is spelt the same as another but has a different meaning is called a **homograph**. The noun *bear*, meaning a big furry mammal, is a homograph of the verb *bear*, meaning to endure or to carry.

7 These words are **homographs**. Think of two different meanings for each word. Write a sentence to show each meaning.

premier: 1. ______________________________

2. ______________________________

cabinet: 1. ______________________________

2. ______________________________

minister: 1. ______________________________

2. ______________________________

8 Add **affixes** to the base word to form related words.

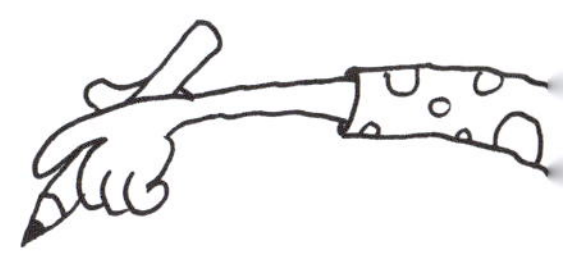

depend ______________________________

democrat ______________________________

oppose ______________________________

federal ______________________________

elect ______________________________

9 Write the correct form of list words to complete the passage.

Most countries are ____________. In these countries, the citizens ____________ their government. In one type of democracy, such as in Australia and Singapore, the government is headed by a prime ____________. In another type of democracy, such as in the United States and France, the government is headed by a ____________. The role of the ____________ is to question government decisions and propose alternative policies.

Answer: c

Spelling Rules! Book 6 (ISBN 9781420236545) © Helen Pearson, Janelle Ho/Macmillan Education Australia

Unit 6 Revision

What is your problem if you are suffering from verbiage?

a you are constantly making up new verbs
b you are allergic to the smell of rotting vegetables
c you use many redundant words

1 Complete the table.

verb	add ed	add ing	noun
persuade	persuaded		
judge		judging	
digest			digestion
admit		admitting	
decide	decided		
oppose		opposing	
pursue			pursuit

2 Write double letters to complete each word.

a _ _ ociation   _ _ rie   pa _ _ enger   permi _ _ ion   cha _ _ enge

c _ _ peration   guarant _ _ d   a _ _ reciation   admi _ _ ion   o _ _ osition

3 Write g or j.

pre _ udice   ad _ acent   refu _ ee   ur _ ent   fra _ ile   jud _ e

4 Write the missing letter or letters that make the s or sh sound.

rejoi _ e   appre _ ia _ _ on   adju _ tment   exten _ _ on   revolu _ _ on

prejudi _ e   exhibi _ _ on   justi _ e   democra _ y   expan _ _ on

5 Rearrange the letters to make an appropriate word.

I received a tintiondisc in the competition. ____________

As time ran out, the teams played with increasing spontraidee. ____________

Japan has the oldest chomanyr in the world. ____________

I'm good at basketball but only gaverea in swimming. ____________

Dad has to go to the doctor to renew his pitcrosprine. ____________

After running the marathon, Cleo was showing signs of exusiohatn. ____________

6 Use the clues to complete the puzzle.

								1			E
							2				E
						3					E
					4				E		
				5						E	
			6						E		
		7	E								
	8	E									
9					E						

1. enemy
2. run away from
3. senior official in a law court
4. needed immediately
5. group of senior government ministers
6. next to
7. Darwin's theory of ____________
8. extreme tiredness
9. working well together

7 Add a suitable prefix.

______digestion ______advantage ______ justice ______decision ______ judge

8 Write the correct form of the word to complete each sentence.

I've got ________________ to go to the late movie on Saturday night.
permit

The ________________ of the riverbank was caused by wind and rain.
erode

Laura asked for Niamh's ________________ in organising the outing.
cooperate

Sherlock Holmes managed great feats of ________________.
detect

We showed our ________________ by giving our teacher some chocolates.
appreciate

All countries pledged to reduce carbon ________________ at the international conference.
emit

9 One word in each sentence is spelt incorrectly. Circle the word and write the correct spelling.

Do flees flee when vets check a sheep's fleece? ________________

The artist made her debue with an exclusive exhibition at the local gallery. ________________

A new extention was built because more students were being enrolled at the school. ________________

Police are trained to detect desception and pursue criminals. ________________

In Australia, the two Houses of Parlament are the Senate and the House of Representatives.

____

Answer: c

Spelling Rules! Book 6 (ISBN 9781420236545) © Helen Pearson, Janelle Ho/Macmillan Education Australia

Unit 7

What are you doing if you are smirking?

a soiling something
b smiling wickedly
c scaring something away

Say Listen Look Understand Remember Practise

permanent	______
terminate	______
persevere	______
mineral	______
several	______
mirth	______
virtual	______
memory	______
temporary	______
curse	______
surplus	______
disturbance	______
yearn	______
adjourn	______
sojourn	______

Tip! The unstressed vowel sound is called a *schwa*. This sound can be written in many ways.

away *animal* *literal* *bitten*
action *kingdom* *evil*

1 Write the missing letters representing the **schwa** sound.

exh _ bit _ _ n   prej _ d _ ce
p _ jam _ s   dev _ stat _ _ n
d _ mocr _ cy   temp _ r _ ry

2 Say aloud each list word that contains **er**. In which two words does **er** make the **schwa** sound?

______ ______

3 Write **er**, **ir**, **or** or **ur**.

v _ _ se   st _ _   w _ _ th
f _ _ ther   mod _ _ n   w _ _ s e
s _ _ face   c _ _ cular   dist _ _ b

4 Underline the letters that make the **er** sound in these words.

journey   search   journal   rehearse   pearl   courtesy

5 Write a list word that is a synonym.

a few ______
end (verb) ______
extra ______
laughter ______

6 Write a list word that is an antonym.

real ______
permanent ______
continue ______
blessing ______

7 Write the correct form of a list verb.

Mrs Quinn ______ her luck when the hail destroyed her garden.
Don't go to sleep now! The train is ______ at the next station.
I overheard Grandma telling my cousin to ______ with his athletics training.

8 Write a list word for each prefix or suffix.

__________ed __________ing im__________ ex__________

9 Add the suffix to make a new word.

virtual + ly → __________

ordinary + ly → __________

temporary + ly → __________

memory + al → __________

terminate + ion → __________

persevere + ance → __________

10 Use all the list words to complete the puzzle.

11 Write about a virtual world. Use as many list words as you can.

Unit 8

What is a hippiater?

a a hip surgeon
b a species of alligator
c a horse doctor

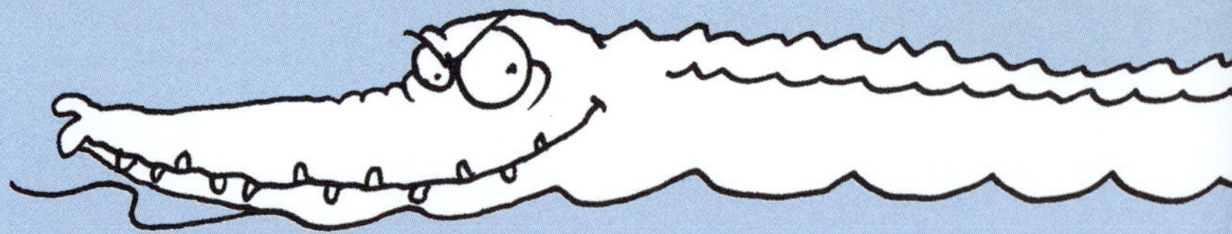

Say Listen Look Understand Remember Practise

electrician	__________
employee	__________
employer	__________
manager	__________
lawyer	__________
pioneer	__________
engineer	__________
translator	__________
sculptor	__________
surgeon	__________
scientist	__________
pharmacist	__________
chef	__________
athlete	__________
chauffeur	__________

1 Complete the table.

occupation	base word
engineer	
manager	
	surgery
	account
	sculpt
scientist	
lawyer	
translator	
	politics

2 Write the two list words that are also French words.

__________ __________

3 Write a list word that fits each group.

nurse anaesthetist
__________ doctor

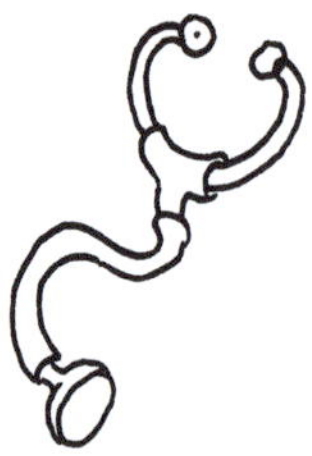

artist
painter
illustrator
____

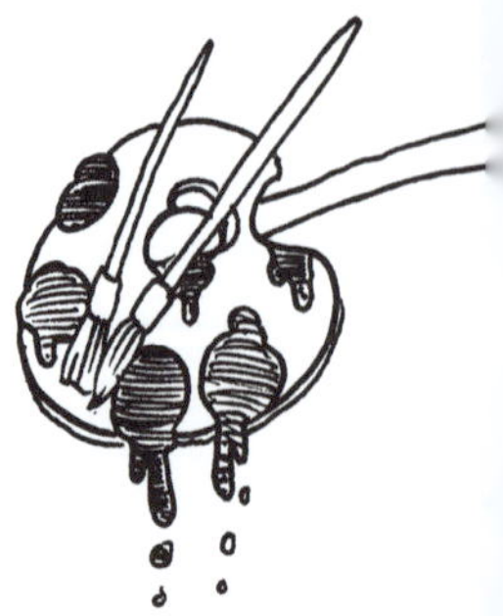

judge __________
prosecutor barrister

physicist
geologist __________
biologist

4 Write the occupation of a person who works in each place.

laboratory	__________	pharmacy	__________
restaurant	__________	car	__________
office	__________	art studio	__________

Spelling Rules! Book 6 (ISBN 9781420236545) © Helen Pearson, Janelle Ho/Macmillan Education Australia

5 The suffix **eer** means "one who works with or is involved in". Write occupations ending in **eer**.

engine ____________ auction ____________

puppet ____________ mountain ____________

6 Use the clue to make a word that matches the meaning.

list word	clue	new word	meaning
chef	add a letter	____________	person in charge
manager	take away a letter	____________	food trough for animals
pioneer	change 3 letters	____________	female lion
surgeon	add a letter	____________	large fish producing caviar

7 Add **er**, **or**, **ian** or **ist** to complete these occupation names. Use a dictionary if you need help.

design______	anaesthet______	music______
curat______	carpent______	zoolog______
millin______	guitar______	librar______
edit______	electric______	invent______
ornitholog______	plumb______	optic______

8 The text has six words that are incorrect. Circle the mistakes. Then write the correct spelling of the words in the boxes.

I enjoy watching the Olympic Games. The venu is usually colourful with the many flags of the participating nations. The atheletes exibit great skill and courage as they persue their dreams and the crowds cheer their appresiation. I feel I am always guranteed great entertainment.

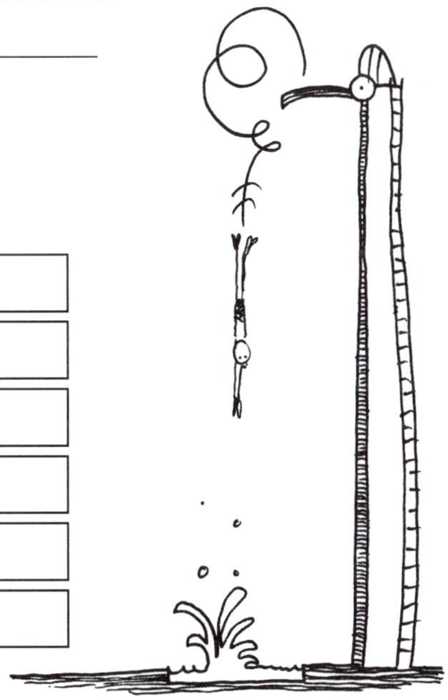

9 *Pioneer* can be both a noun and a verb. Write a sentence for each meaning of the word.

pioneer (noun): ________________________________

____

pioneer (verb): ________________________________

____

Answer: c

Unit 9

Risibility is the ability to:

a rise early
b laugh easily
c rotate your wrists

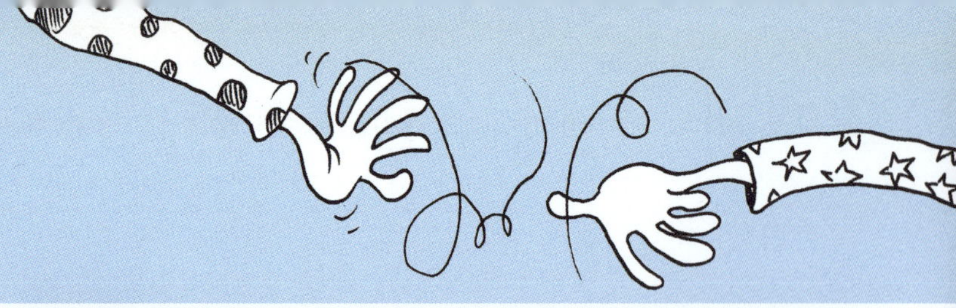

Say Listen Look Understand Remember Practise

ability ____________
stability ____________
durability ____________
probability ____________
acceptability ____________
predictability ____________
respectability ____________
changeability ____________
availability ____________
irritability ____________
possibility ____________
visibility ____________
flexibility ____________
responsibility ____________
accessibility ____________

Tip! Words ending in **ible** and **able** are adjectives. These words may also add **ity** as a second suffix.
Adding **ity** changes the adjective to a noun.

1 Write the list words ending in **ibility**. Then write the adjectival form.

noun	adjective

2 Write the list words ending in **ability**. Then write the adjectival form.

noun	adjective

noun	adjective

3 Write the list word in which silent **e** has been kept when the suffixes are added to the base word.

____

Another word that keeps silent **e** is *traceability*. Why do these words keep the silent **e**?

____

Spelling Rules! Book 6 (ISBN 9781420236545) © Helen Pearson, Janelle Ho/Macmillan Education Australia

4 Use each clue to find a smaller word within a list word. Write the small word and the list word.

clue	answer	list word
the opposite of *off*	____________	____________________
what thieves do	____________	____________________
the colour of anger or embarrassment	____________	____________________
what you do to show off your muscles	____________	____________________

5 Add **un**, **im**, **in** or **ir** to make an antonym.

_____flexibility _____possiblity _____predictability _____responsibility

_____reliability _____ability _____stability _____plausibility

6 Write list words.

Our coach thinks that Rahim has the ______________ to play for Australia one day.

Lili avoids ______________ and constantly surprises us with new magic tricks.

Our bushwalk was cancelled due to the ______________ of a thunderstorm.

Buster, our dog, has been bad-tempered recently. Our vet discovered that his ______________ was due to an infection in his ear.

Janie's ______________ this week is to clean the board; Lucas's is to turn off the lights and fans.

Animals are migratory if the ______________ of food and water is not constant.

______________ to buildings is important for people with mobility problems.

7 Make a noun from each adjective. What does each noun mean?

	noun	meaning
audible	______________	______________________________
invincible	______________	______________________________
durable	______________	______________________________
feasible	______________	______________________________
manoeuvrable	______________	______________________________

Answer: b

Unit 10

Continuous and **contiguous** are often confused. What does contiguous mean?

a the contents of a tin
b including tigers
c adjacent

Say Listen Look Understand Remember Practise	
accent	________
ascent	________
device	________
devise	________
cemetery	________
symmetry	________
stationery	________
stationary	________
bizarre	________
bazaar	________
affect	________
breath	________
excess	________
descent	________
wander	________

1 The words in each pair are easily confused. Underline the part of each word that sounds different.

accent	descent	symmetry
ascent	decent	cemetery
breath	wander	excess
breathe	wonder	access

Tip! The **etymology** of a word tells us where the word comes from and what its original meaning was.

2 **Bizarre** and **bazaar** are often confused. Write the correct word in each sentence. Use a dictionary if you need help. Then write the correct words to complete the final sentence.

__________ is a French word meaning odd or fantastic.

__________ is an old Persian word meaning market.

I saw a __________ statue at the __________.

Tip! Some confusing pairs of words are the verb and noun form of the same word. For example, *advise* is the verb while *advice* is the noun. A useful mnemonic for advise/advice is that the verb **advise** contains the verb **is** and the noun **advice** contains the noun **ice**.

3 Write in the brackets whether each word is a noun or a verb. Use a dictionary if you need help. Then write the correct word in each sentence.

practise (________)
practice (________)

I __________ the piano every day.
Sam fell over at basketball __________.

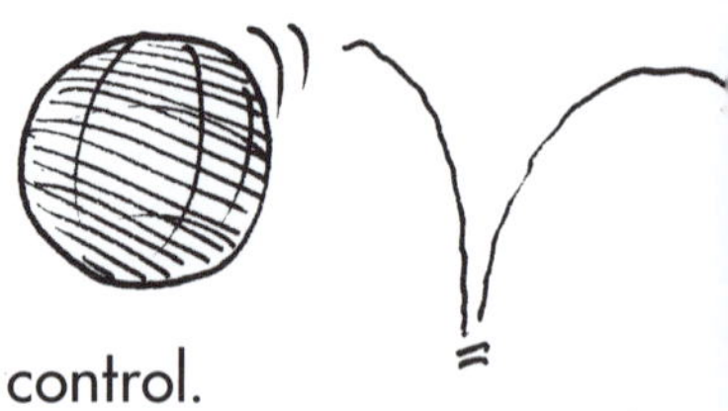

devise (________)
device (________)

Dad's favourite __________ is the remote control.
For our project we have to __________ a weighing scale.

advise (________)
advice (________)

Can you __________ me about how to use the equipment?
Some people don't accept __________ well.

4 Draw a line to match each word to its meaning. Then use one of the words in your own sentence.

excess	extra
access	way through

____

desert	sweet food eaten at the end of a meal
dessert	an extremely dry place

____

stationary	not moving
stationery	things used for writing

____

affect	to make a difference
effect	the result of an action

____

5 One word in each sentence is wrong. The correct word may be a homophone or a similar-sounding word. Circle the incorrect word and write the word correctly.

Jonah pulled a mussel while running in the 100 metre race. ______________

It's rained every day this week accept Tuesday. ______________

I wander whether my aunt will come to visit today. ______________

How long can you hold your breathe underwater? ______________

Pia's mother has lived here for many years but she still has an ascent. ______________

The hailstorm had a devastating affect. ______________

6 Write the other homophone or homophones, then use each set of homophones in a sentence.

lesson ______________

____

____

medal ______________

____

____

threw ______________

____

____

Answer: c

Spelling Rules! Book 6 (ISBN 9781420236545) © Helen Pearson, Janelle Ho/Macmillan Education Australia

Unit 11

What is trichology?

a the science of hair and its diseases
b the knowledge of three-sided objects
c the study of tricks

Say Listen Look Understand Remember Practise	
environment	
rainforest	
pollution	
greenhouse	
climate	
recycle	
ozone	
ecology	
irrigation	
conservation	
deforestation	
flora	
fauna	
sustainable	
atmosphere	

1 Write the affixes used in the list words.

suffixes ______ ______
______ ______

prefixes ______
______

2 Write the base words.

pollution ______
irrigation ______
conservation ______
sustainable ______
recycle ______
emission ______

3 Write the list words which are compound words.

______ ______

Tip! Prefixes and suffixes (affixes) add to the meaning of a base word.
de + *forest* + *ation* = the process of getting rid of forests

4 Write the meanings of these words. Use a dictionary if you need help.

reforestation: ______
unsustainable: ______
pollutants: ______

5 Use each clue to find a smaller word within a list word. Write the small word and the list word.

clue	answer	list word
a 3D shape		
a number		
a discoloured patch		
where a train stops		

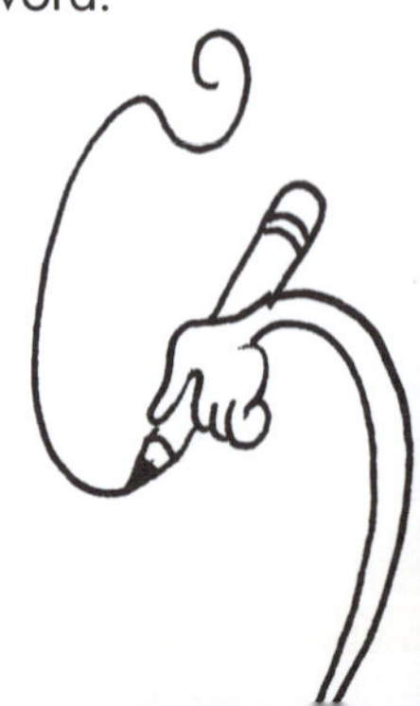

Spelling Rules! Book 6 (ISBN 9781420236545) © Helen Pearson, Janelle Ho/Macmillan Education Australia

6 Use some of the letters in each list word to make a three-letter, a four-letter and a five-letter word.

	environment	irrigation	sustainable
3 letters	______	______	______
4 letters	______	______	______
5 letters	______	______	______

7 Use list words to complete the diagram. Briefly explain the diagram.

______

+

______

→ the ______ effect → ______ change and rising sea levels

______

______

______

Tip! **logy** is a word element that means *science* or *the study of*.
bio (living things) + *logy* → *biology*

8 Use a dictionary to find the meaning of each word. Write the meaning, then use the word in a sentence.

ecology: ______

______

geology: ______

______

zoology: ______

______

meteorology: ______

______

9 Use a list word to name each category. Add more examples.

______: trees, shrubs, grass, ______, ______

______: mammals, insects, fish, ______, ______

______: hose, dam, water pipe, ______, ______

Answer: a

Unit 12 Revision

What is a snotter?

a a rope attached to a ship's mast
b a person with a cold
c a sick pig

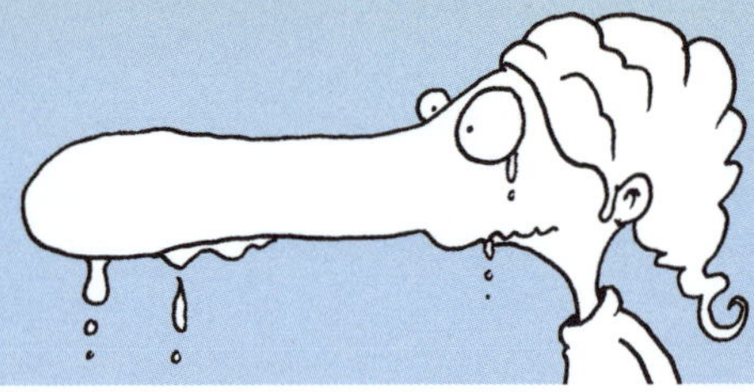

1 Write ir, er, or or ur.

s___face desp___ation p___severe w___th s___geon

sculpt___ cons___vation mem___y v___tual gov___n___

2 Write the noun form.

disturb ______________ decide ______________

responsible ______________ accept ______________

pollute ______________ translate ______________

irrigate ______________ able ______________

3 Write an occupation associated with each picture.

 ______________  ______________

 ______________  ______________

4 Use a prefix to make the antonym.

permanent ______________ certainty ______________ flexibility ______________

sustainable ______________ possibility ______________ stability ______________

5 Use each word in a sentence.

affect ____

effect ____

6 Colour the correct word.

Fireworks have a terrible | affect | effect | on my dog, who howls and whimpers.

Dad's taking me to buy some | stationary | stationery | for my project.

I had to | practice | practise | for weeks before I could hold my | breath | breathe | long enough to swim across the pool underwater.

Alita and her friends love to go to the Saturday | bazaar | bizarre |.

7 Rewrite each sentence using one word to replace the underlined word or phrase.

We really admire Aoki because he never stops trying.

____

Airports must close if fog reduces the ability to see.

____

We put our empty bottles in the yellow bin so that they can be made into something else.

____

The world has to be careful about getting rid of all the forests, or our way of life may not be able to be sustained.

____

8 Complete the tables.

noun	adjective
responsibility	
	possible
	flexible
visibility	

noun	adjective
	stable
availability	
	probable
predictability	

9 Write the correct form of the verb to complete each sentence.

Our team captain later ______________ (accept) responsibility for mixing up the time of our match.

Yesterday, Alan ______________ (admit) that he used to believe in bunyips.

Everyone had to ______________ (cooperate) to complete the obstacle course.

Were you ______________ (disturb) by the thunderstorm last night?

______________ (change) my shirt at half time definitely helped me play better.

10 Write about how recycling helps the environment.

____

____

____

Answer: a

Spelling Rules! Book 6 (ISBN 9781420236545) © Helen Pearson, Janelle Ho/Macmillan Education Australia

Unit 13

What does it mean to ride pill**ion**?

a to be a passenger on a motorcycle
b to deliver medicines in a van
c to carry pillows on a bike

Say Listen Look Understand Remember Practise

opin**ion**	______
tuit**ion**	______
rat**ion**al	______
occas**ion**al	______
pr**ior**	______
sen**ior**	______
super**ior**	______
infer**ior**	______
exter**ior**	______
poster**ior**	______
med**ian**	______
all**ian**ce	______
rad**ian**t	______
pecul**iar**	______
d**iar**rhoea	______

1 Write a list word that rhymes.

fire ______
defiance ______
ignition ______
gradient ______

2 Write the list word that is an antonym.

junior ______
inferior ______
irrational ______
interior ______
frequent ______

3 Write the list word that is a synonym.

union ______
shining ______
strange ______
previous ______

Tip! *Interior, exterior, posterior* and *anterior* describe different positions. The first syllable indicates the position.

4 Complete each sentence.

If *postpone* means *put off until later*, then **post** means ______.
If *antenatal* means *before birth*, then **ante** means ______.
If *external* means *outside*, then **ex** means ______.
If *internal* means *inside*, then **in** means ______.

5 Draw a line to match each word to its meaning.

interior	before
exterior	inside
anterior	behind
posterior	outside

Spelling Rules! Book 6 (ISBN 9781420236545) © Helen Pearson, Janelle Ho/Macmillan Education Australia

Tip!

A mnemonic helps you remember something tricky.
*Bring your **ears** to reh**ears**als.*
*There is **a rat** in sep**arat**e.*

6 Make up a mnemonic to help you remember the spelling of *diarrhoea*.

____

Tip!

Many of the list words add **ity** to make the noun.
prior → priority

7 Make a new word by changing and/or adding a letter. Use it in a sentence.

inferior ____
median ____
g + radiant ____
rational + e ____

8 Add **ity** to make the noun.

prior	____________	senior	____________
inferior	____________	peculiar	____________
superior	____________	familiar	____________

9 Write list words to complete the puzzle. Write your own clue for each word.

Across

1. ______________________
3. ______________________
7. ______________________
8. ______________________
9. ______________________

Down

2. ______________________
3. ______________________
4. ______________________
5. ______________________
6. ______________________

Unit 14

What is a pest**le**?

a a pest elimination service
b a club-shaped tool used to grind spices
c a small child being a nuisance

Say Listen Look Understand Remember Practise

optic**al** ____________
practic**al** ____________
skelet**al** ____________
seri**al** ____________
gradu**al** ____________
benefici**al** ____________
sequenti**al** ____________
especi**al**ly ____________
essenti**al**ly ____________
exc**el** ____________
reb**el** ____________
parall**el** ____________
partic**le** ____________
chort**le** ____________
vehic**le** ____________

1 Write the list words that have a hard **c** sound, as in *clear*.

____________ ____________
____________ ____________

2 Complete the table.

base word	list word
sequence	
	essentially
benefit	
	serial
skeleton	
	practical

Tip! **Serial** and **cereal** are homophones.

3 Write *serial* or *cereal* to complete each sentence.

I have ____________ for breakfast every morning, except on weekends.
The ____________ numbers of the stolen banknotes were published in the newspaper.
I can't wait to see the next instalment of the television ____________.
Wheat, rye, oats and maize are all kinds of ____________.

4 Use the words to label the pictures.

abdominal aural dental spinal optical nasal

Spelling Rules! Book 6 (ISBN 9781420236545) © Helen Pearson, Janelle Ho/Macmillan Education Australia

5 Write as many words as you can ending in **tle**. Circle the word if the **t** is silent.

____

____

Tip! **Metal** and **mettle** are homophones.

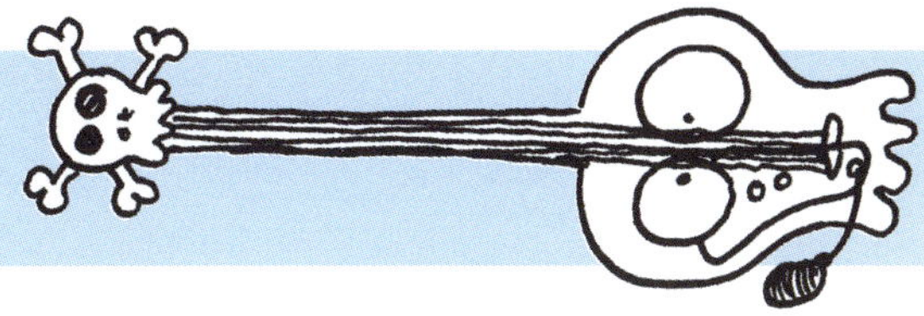

6 Use a dictionary to find the meaning of **metal** and **mettle**. Use each word in a sentence.

mettle: ____

metal: ____

Rule! If a noun ends in **ce**, change the **ce** to **ti** before adding **al** to make the adjective.

confidence → *confidential*

Exceptions: *office* → *official*   *practice* → *practical*

7 Add **al**.

essence → ____________

preference → ____________

substance → ____________

sequence → ____________

palace → ____________

consequence → ____________

8 Write a list word to match each meaning.

in particular ____________

lines that are always the same distance apart ____________

progressing slowly ____________

something of a very small size ____________

something with wheels for transportation ____________

9 Write the correct form of the verb to complete each sentence.

The hero in the story ____________ against his boss when he had to commit a crime.
rebel

The champion has been ____________ in her sport for many years.
excel

I couldn't stop ____________ when I heard the joke.
chortle

The plan lacked ____________.
practical

Ha ha ha ha ha ha ha!

Answer: b

Unit 15

What does vertiginous mean?

a vertical
b whirling
c a virtual reality game show

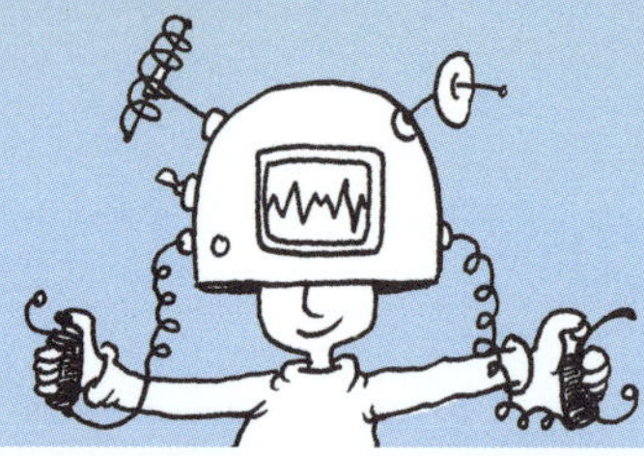

Say Listen Look Understand Remember Practise

wondrous	
disastrous	
humorous	
hazardous	
miraculous	
indigenous	
mysterious	
suspicious	
envious	
rebellious	
ferocious	
voracious	
precarious	
advantageous	
spontaneous	

Tip! Sometimes the base word changes when **ous** is added.

1 Look at the base word. Write the related list word, then state the change to the base word.

base word	list word	change to base word
wonder		delete ____
disaster		delete ____
humour		delete ____
miracle		change le to ___

2 Write the two list words that have no change to the base word when **ous** is added.

______________ ______________

Rule! If the base word ends in **ce** or **y**, change **e** or **y** to **i** before adding **ous**.
fury → furious *vice → vicious*

3 Add **ous**.

study → ______________ grace → ______________ glory → ______________
envy → ______________ mystery → ______________ luxury → ______________
malice → ______________ space → ______________ fury → ______________

Rule! If the base word ends in **e**, drop the **e** before adding **ous**. *fame → famous*
Exception: some words ending in **ge** *courage → courageous*

4 Add **ous**.

ridicule → ______________ courage → ______________ outrage → ______________
carnivore → ______________ nerve → ______________ advantage → ______________

Spelling Rules! Book 6 (ISBN 9781420236545) © Helen Pearson, Janelle Ho/Macmillan Education Australia

5 Write list words.

We never know what's going to happen when we stay with Grandma. We have great fun and my friends are quite ________________. Once she woke us in the middle of the night to watch a meteor shower. It was a ________________ sight. Another time, she thought her neighbours were behaving in a ________________ manner, so we followed them for a while as if we were detectives. She has a dog who looks ________________ but will eat bits of toast out of your hand.

Tip! **Similes** describe something by comparing it to something else using *like* or *as*.
The old building looked as precarious as a house of cards.

6 Write a simile for each word: *suspicious, precarious, marvellous.*

____

____

____

7 Write the list word that is a synonym. What does the final word mean?

										O	U	S	jealous
										O	U	S	funny
										O	U	S	greedy
										O	U	S	aboriginal
										O	U	S	impulsive
										O	U	S	favourable
C	O	N	S	C	I	E	N	T	I	O	U	S	________________

8 Use each clue to find a smaller word within a list word. Write the small word and the list word.

clue	answer	list word
something you can ring	________________	________________
a browning of the skin	________________	________________
first in a race	________________	________________
a passenger vehicle	________________	________________
to sing without words	________________	________________
a delivery vehicle	________________	________________
move soil with a spade	________________	________________

Answer: b

Unit 16

What does the word element **neo** mean?

a nil
b new
c a broken neon light

Say Listen Look Understand Remember Practise

novel
novelty
novice
innovate
innovation
vocal
vocabulary
advocate
vociferous
invoke
provoke
notice
notify
annotate
reminisce

1 Sort the list words into adjectives, verbs and nouns. Some words may belong to more than one group.

verbs

nouns

adjectives

Tip! **Etymology** is the study of the origin of words. Most English words have Old English, Latin or Greek origins. Synonyms often have different origins. For example, *new* is from Old English, while *novel* is from Latin.

The Latin origins for the list words are:

nova = new *vox* = voice *notare* = note *reminisci* = remember.

2 Group the list words.

related to **voice**:

related to **note**:

related to **remember**:

related to **new**:

Spelling Rules! Book 6 (ISBN 9781420236545) © Helen Pearson, Janelle Ho/Macmillan Education Australia

3 Using the word origin as a clue, write a list word to match each definition.

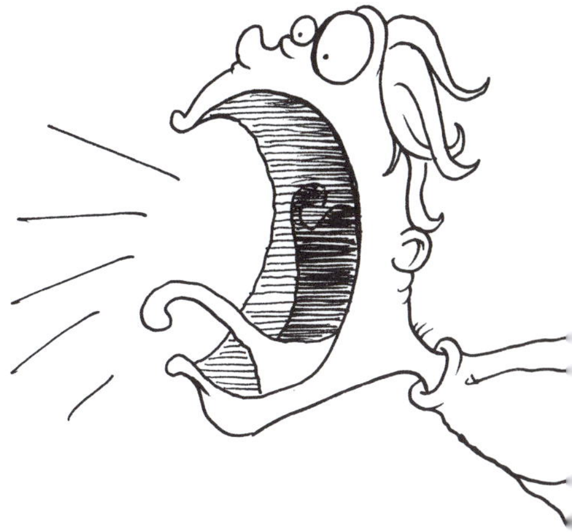

speaking with a loud, fierce voice ______________

someone new and inexperienced ______________

to produce something new ______________

to call forth ______________

to make notes ______________

to remember the past ______________

to speak on someone's behalf ______________

something new and unusual ______________

4 These words belong to the same word family as list words. Use each word in a sentence to show its meaning. Choose another list word and write a related word and sentence of your own.

renovation: ______________________________

notorious: ______________________________

revoke: ______________________________

reminiscent: ______________________________

______________ ______________________________

Tip! **Novel** is a homograph. It has two different meanings.

5 Write a definition for each meaning of *novel*.

novel (noun) = ______________________________

novel (adjective) = ______________________________

6 Use a list word to complete each title. Make up a title and author of your own.

A Complete ______________ by B Ginner

______________ No More! by I Forget

______________ in the Home by Han D Man

The ______________ Speaker by IM Noisy

Creating a Great ______________ by Rider Book

______________________ by ______________

Answer: b

Etymology nova, vox, notare, reminisci; homograph novel

Unit 17

A peri**scope** is:

a a gourmet plum
b a viewing device on a submarine
c a device to measure the perimeter of an area

Say Listen Look Understand Remember Practise

solution	______
toxic	______
method	______
experiment	______
acid	______
alkaline	______
temperature	______
evaporate	______
thermometer	______
theory	______
equipment	______
chemical	______
microscope	______
hypothesis	______
laboratory	______

1 Divide these list words into syllables. Underline the syllable that is stressed in each word.

method	alkaline
evaporate	equipment
microscope	hypothesis
temperature	acid

Rule! **ic** is a less common suffix that changes a noun to an adjective. The base word usually changes when **ic** is added.

tragedy → *tragic*

2 Add **ic** to make the adjective. The base word may change. Use a dictionary if you need help.

noun	adjective
base	
acid	
toxin	
science	
horror	

Tip! In a compound word, both parts can be used independently. Some words are not compound words, but consist of two separate word elements. **Scope** and **meter** can act as words and as word elements. As word elements, **scope** refers to a viewing instrument and **meter** to a measuring instrument.

3 Use a dictionary to find the meaning of the word element and the whole word.

micro = ______ microscope = ______
thermo = ______ thermometer = ______

Write other words you know that use these word elements.

scope: ______
meter: ______

4 Write the correct form of a list word to complete each sentence.

What usually makes people sick are ________________ creatures called viruses and bacteria.

When you bake a cake, it is very important to follow the ________________ given in the recipe.

Some ________________ are poisonous. Bottles containing dangerous materials are usually labelled ________________.

My teacher believes that any place can be a ________________. She encourages us to carry out ________________ to test things out. I am going to test my ________________ that the room temperature affects how quickly a slice of apple goes brown.

5 Use list words to complete the puzzle.

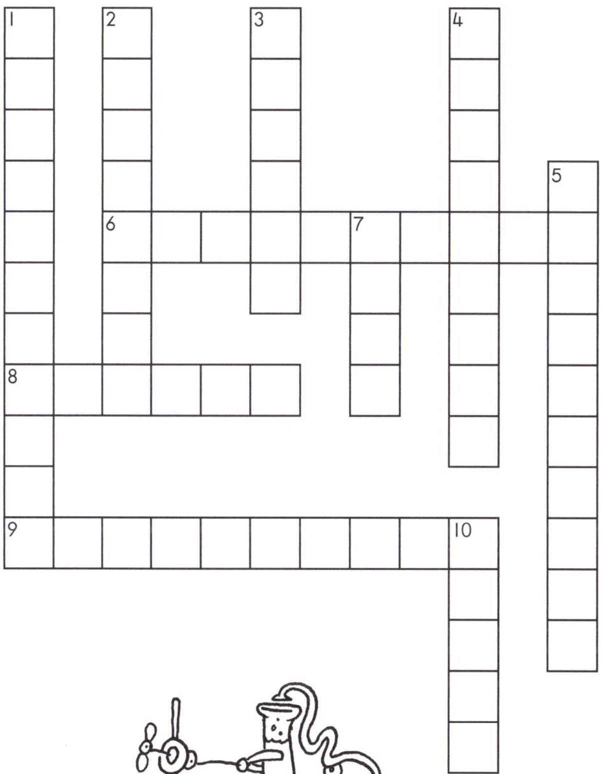

Across

6. a room in which experiments are performed
8. a way of explaining what is observed
9. a way of testing a theory

Down

1. a measure of how hot or cold something is
2. a solution is either neutral, acidic or ________
3. good experiments follow the scientific ________
4. to convert a liquid into a gas
5. what is tested during an experiment
7. vinegar is a common ________
10. poisonous

6 Write whether these word pairs are synonyms or antonyms.

acidic/alkaline ________________

evaporation/condensation ________________

hypothesis/theory ________________

equipment/apparatus ________________

theoretical/practical ________________

problem/difficulty ________________

Unit 18 Revision

The word quadrumanous is used to describe:

a lions that have four manes
b animals that use four feet as hands
c animals that have four teeth for eating

1 Complete the tables.

noun	adjective
disaster	
advantage	
humour	
mystery	
skeleton	
essence	
practice	

verb	noun
edit	
equip	
solve	

verb	adjective
radiate	
benefit	
rebel	

2 Write words that follow each rule.

Remove silent **e** from the base word before adding a suffix.

____

Change the final **y** to **i** before adding a suffix.

____

Keep the **e** so **g** stays soft when adding a suffix.

____

3 Write the correct form of the verb to complete each sentence.

Dad was ________________ that he had jury duty next month.
notify

Uncle Carlos ________________ against all the rules when he was young but now he's a police inspector!
rebel

I love the cakes at Pierre's Patisserie because they are always ________________ with new flavours.
experiment

Did you know that if you drink too much water, you can get water ________________?
poison

Because the water ________________ as soon as it hit the pan, I knew the pan was hot.
evaporate

When Dana is amused, she doesn't just laugh, she ________________.
chortle

Spelling Rules! Book 6 (ISBN 9781420236545) © Helen Pearson, Janelle Ho/Macmillan Education Australia

4 Use a word you have learnt to complete each sentence.

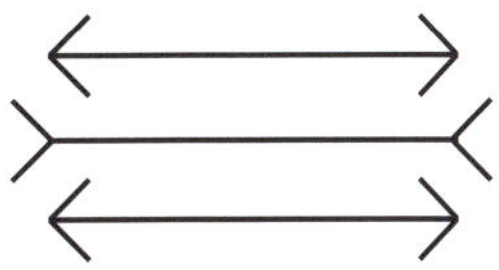

In this diagram, the ______________ lines look like they are of unequal lengths, but they are actually the same length. It is an ______________ illusion.

Anton van Leeuwenhoek was the first person to observe bacteria under a ______________.

You must take precautions when handling ______________ chemicals.

The best way to increase your ______________ is to read a lot.

A stomach bug gave Ramon a bad case of ______________.

Cherie is always happy to give her ______________ on any issue.

Tip! When two or more words start with the same sound, it is called **alliteration**.

5 Write a second word so that each pair is an example of alliteration.

hideous ______________	______________ occasion
peculiar ______________	______________ vehicle
spontaneous ______________	______________ laboratory

6 Write a word to name each category.

	car, truck, tractor, van
	Wheaty Flakes, Rice Pops, Corn Puffs, muesli
	chlorine, ammonia, sodium chloride, fluoride

7 Proofread this text. The text has six words that are incorrect. Circle the mistakes. Then write the correct spelling of the words in the boxes.

The scientist was carrying out an experiment in her laborratory. She had a hypothises to test. Her method was to combine an acid and an alkali in different proportions and measure the temperature at which the solution boiled with a digital thermommeter. She wandered if the results would confirm her theorey that newtral solutions had the highest boiling point.

Answer: b

Spelling Rules! Book 6 (ISBN 9781420236545) © Helen Pearson, Janelle Ho/Macmillan Education Australia

Unit 19

Flocculation is what happens when:

a music makes you sway from side to side
b flocks of sheep gather
c things are formed in a woolly mass

Say Listen Look Understand Remember Practise

satisfaction ______
definition ______
repetition ______
conversation ______
alteration ______
continuation ______
declaration ______
cancellation ______
explanation ______
exclamation ______
variation ______
multiplication ______
application ______
identification ______
notification ______

1 Complete the table.

verb	noun
satisfy	
define	
	cancellation
	declaration
	exclamation
alter	
	repetition
	continuation

Rule! To add **ion** to a base word ending in **y**, change the **y** to **i** and add **cation**.
multiply → multiplication
Some exceptions: *vary → variation*
satisfy → satisfaction

2 Complete the tables.

base word	add ion	base word	add ion
apply		notify	
multiply		magnify	
identify		vilify	

3 Say the list words out loud, then complete the statements.

All of the list words except one have ______ more syllables than their base words.
The list word that is the exception is ______.

4 Write the noun form for each verb. Say each pair aloud.

describe → ______ classify → ______ define → ______

Q: What happens to the stress on the final syllable? ______

______

5 **Convert** and **converse** both form a noun ending in **ion**. Write the nouns, then use each one in a sentence. Use a dictionary if you need help.

convert → ____________

____

converse → ____________

____

6 Use the clues to complete the puzzle.

												Clue
									I	O	N	all talk and no ____________
									I	O	N	learning with a tutor
									I	O	N	The judge's ____________ is final.
									I	O	N	antonym of acceptance
									I	O	N	what someone makes when they accuse you of something
									I	O	N	What is your ____________ for being late?
									I	O	N	document that informs you of something

> **Tip!**
> An **abbreviation** is either a short form of a word, or the first letter of each word in a phrase.
> *government → govt* *United States of America → USA*
> An **acronym** is a special kind of abbreviation. In an acronym, the abbreviation is pronounced as a whole word.
> *AIDS* *PIN*

7 Write the abbreviated name of each organisation. Circle the abbreviations that are acronyms.

United Nations Educational, Scientific and Cultural Organisation ____________
Organisation of Petroleum Exporting Countries ____________
Royal Society for the Prevention of Cruelty to Animals ____________
North Atlantic Treaty Organisation ____________
National Aeronautic and Space Administration ____________
Asia-Pacific Economic Cooperation group ____________

8 What is odd about these phrases that contain an abbreviation?

ATM machine HIV virus PIN number

____

____

____

Answer: c

Unit 20

An aviary is where:

a aircraft are designed
b honey is harvested
c birds are kept

Say Listen Look Understand Remember Practise

library ____________
salary ____________
imaginary ____________
secondary ____________
summary ____________
documentary ____________
gallery ____________
grocery ____________
jewellery ____________
forgery ____________
category ____________
exploratory ____________
accusatory ____________
dormitory ____________
laundry ____________

1 Complete the table.

base word	list word
	imaginary
second	
sum	
document	
	jewellery
	forgery
explore	
	accusatory

Tip! Some words can be pronounced in two ways and in one way, a syllable is not pronounced.
For example, *dormitory* can be pronounced as *daw-muh-tuh-ry* or *daw-muh-try*.
A syllable that is not pronounced is **elided**.

2 These words can be pronounced in two ways. Circle the syllable that can be elided.

category   secretary   jewellery   desperate

Tip! These pairs of words are sometimes confused.
salary = money paid for regular work
celery = a crisp green vegetable
summary = a brief presentation of facts
summery = like summer, or to do with summer

3 Write the correct word to complete each sentence.

I love ____________ because of its crunchy texture.
My parents are saving part of their ____________ each month so we can buy a new car.
The blurb on the back of a book gives a brief ____________ of what the book is about.
It was an autumn day, but the warm breeze made it feel ____________.

4 Add **ary**, **ery** or **ory**.

diction____   bound____   lavat____   secret____   laborat____   the____
hist____   imag____   lott____   burgl____   necess____   volunt____

5 Write a list word to complete each advertising slogan.

PUT YOURSELF IN THE PICTURE! Visit the National Portrait ______________ today.

Drop in for a word or two with us at your local ______________.

THE FASTEST FOOD OF ALL! Peel a banana from Jo's Green ______________.

Z Z Z z z z z

____

THE HOME OF SLEEP

There's no present like the time! Watch out for specials at Clocks 'n' Gems ______________.

6 Use **stationary** or **stationery** to complete each sentence.

The doors will not open until the bus is ______________.

Where's the cheapest place to buy the ______________ I need for school?

Some satellites are geo______________ in their orbit.

7 Each small word can be found inside a list word. Use the list words to complete the story.

sum	tar	all	rat	for

Last night I watched a ______________ on an exhibition at the State Art ______________. The commentator was giving a detailed ______________ of each artist's life, when what I was interested in were the paintings. But it got interesting when the commentator began an ______________ conversation with an artist he suspected of ______________.

8 Proofread this text. The text has five words that are incorrect. Circle the mistakes. Then write the correct spelling of the words in the boxes.

I love books, and one day I'd like to work in a libary. I think I'd enjoy putting each new book into its correct category. I'm not sure what the salery would be. To become a librarian you have to finish secondory school first, and then go to university. I think I'll try doing work experience in a library first, to make sure that the good points aren't just imaginery!

Answer: c

Unit 21

A **poly**glot is:

a someone who eats parrots
b a figure with many angles and sides
c a person who speaks many languages

Say Listen Look Understand Remember Practise

monopoly ____________
monolith ____________
monotonous ____________
monosyllabic ____________
multiple ____________
multipurpose ____________
multimedia ____________
multicultural ____________
multilingual ____________
polygon ____________
polyphonic ____________
omnivore ____________
omnipresent ____________
omnipotent ____________
omniscient ____________

Tip! A **word element** is a part of a word that can only be used in combination with another part of a word.

1 Draw a line to match the word element with its meaning.

mono	all
multi	one
omni	many

Which of the word elements above means the same as **poly**?

____

Tip! **Multi** is Latin in origin and **poly** is Greek. Early Greek expertise in mathematics and science means that many words in these areas start with **poly**, not **multi**.

polygon *polyester*

2 Underline the syllable that is stressed.

monolith	multiple	omnivore	polygon
monotonous	multicultural	omnivorous	polyphonic

3 Write words beginning with these word elements.

mono / bi / multi → lingual

____
____
____

mono / tri / poly → syllabic

____
____
____

tri / quadru / multi → ple

____
____
____

Spelling Rules! Book 6 (ISBN 9781420236545) © Helen Pearson, Janelle Ho/Macmillan Education Australia

4 Use a dictionary to find the meaning of each word. Write the meaning, then name some animals in each category. Add the suffix **ous** and use the word as an adjective in a sentence.

herbivore = ____________________

carnivore = ____________________

omnivore = ____________________

Tip! Mrs Malaprop was a character in a play who continually mixed up similar-sounding words. These "slips of the tongue" are now called *malapropisms*.

5 Circle the malapropism in each sentence, then write the correct word.

I don't like *Rap 'n' Roar's* latest song. It's got a strong rhythm but it gets monogamous. ____________

Triangles and squares are examples of polyglots. ____________

Big Brother is omnivorous: he knows everything. ____________

We use the multiparty hall for basketball, badminton and assemblies. ____________

There are multiplied ways of doing this. You just need to choose one. ____________

My brother's favourite board game is Monotony. ____________

Now write a deliberate malapropism of your own.

____

6 Monopoly is one of the most popular board games in the world. Explain how it got its name. Use a dictionary if you need help.

____

Unit 22

A heckel**phone** is:
a a loud heckler
b a noisy telephone
c a musical instrument

Say Listen Look Understand Remember Practise

symphony	______
phonetic	______
microphone	______
cacophony	______
synonym	______
antonym	______
pseudonym	______
anonymous	______
sympathy	______
empathy	______
telepathy	______
majesty	______
majority	______
magnify	______
magnificent	______

1 Write a list word that rhymes.

athletic ______
priority ______
synonymous ______

2 Write a list word that contains the smaller word.

net	cop
______	______
crop	ice
______	______
jest	one
______	______
pat	cent
______	______
______	or
______	______

3 Write whether these word pairs are synonyms or antonyms. Then write your own examples of synonyms and antonyms.

	synonyms or antonyms?	**your examples**
majority/most	______	______
cheerful/gloomy	______	______

4 Write a word that has the same underlined word element.

<u>micro</u>phone ______ <u>maj</u>esty ______ <u>tele</u>pathy ______

5 Circle the meaning of each word element.

micro	loud	small	measure
magni	great	royal	magic
tele	sound	sender	far away

Spelling Rules! Book 6 (ISBN 9781420236545) © Helen Pearson, Janelle Ho/Macmillan Education Australia

6 The meaning of each word element is given. L or G shows whether the word is from Latin or Greek. Write the list word that combines these word elements.

tele G: *far away*	+	patheia G: *feeling*	=	__________
kako G: *bad*	+	phone G: *sound*	=	__________
syn G: *together*	+	onyma G: *name*	=	__________
anti G: *opposite*	+	onyma G: *name*	=	__________
pseudo G: *false*	+	onyma G: *name*	=	__________
em L: *in*	+	patheia G: *feeling*	=	__________
poly G: *many*	+	phonic G: *sound*	=	__________

7 Circle the malapropism in each sentence and write the correct word.

The magician claimed he used mental telegraphy to communicate with his assistant. __________

The kidnapper sent a synonymous letter demanding a huge ransom. __________

The authority of the class voted to play volleyball in the gym. __________

Sam wears glasses to modify the text on his laptop. __________

8 Rewrite each sentence using the correct form of a list word to make it shorter.

Dictionaries often use an alphabet in which symbols replace letters to represent pronunciation.

____

Mrs Jenkins assured us that she was experiencing the same sad feelings that we were.

____

Being on stage is scary because the silence makes every mistake seem bigger.

____

Answer: c

Etymology: phone, onyma, patheia, magnus

Unit 23

WHO is the abbreviation for:

a World Health Organisation
b World Horticultural Organisation
c Wild Horses in the Outback

Say Listen Look Understand Remember Practise

medicine ____
bacteria ____
virus ____
pregnant ____
fracture ____
organ ____
influenza ____
abdomen ____
intestine ____
capsule ____
appendix ____
vaccination ____
immunisation ____
pneumonia ____
stethoscope ____

1 Write list words to complete the table.

Category	Examples
	antibiotics, aspirin, ____
medical equipment	syringe, thermometer, ____
	heart, lungs, ____
illnesses	bronchitis, tonsillitis, ____

2 Write list words to answer the questions.

Which word has a silent letter? ____

Which words end in the same vowel sound?

____ ____ ____

Which words have a soft **c** sound?

____ ____

Which words contain double letters?

____ ____ ____

3 Use each clue to find a smaller word within a list word. Write the small word and the list word.

clue	answer	list word
an assessment task		
a shape like a hemisphere		
a type of hat		
a strong but tiny insect		
a tool for writing		
to play a part		
rested on a chair		

Spelling Rules! Book 6 (ISBN 9781420236545) © Helen Pearson, Janelle Ho/Macmillan Education Australia

Tip! The word **organ** is a homograph. The word **appendix** is also a homograph. Each word has two very different meanings.

4 Write sentences to show the different meanings of *organ* and *appendix*. Use a dictionary if you need help.

organ 1. ______________________________

2. ______________________________

appendix 1. ______________________________

2. ______________________________

5 Which word does not belong? Why not?

chronic fracture medical stomach muscle ache bacteria

____

6 Write what each abbreviation stands for. Circle the abbreviations that are acronyms.

flu	______________	CF	______________
AIDS	______________	ADD	______________
MS	______________	SIDS	______________

7 Each sentence contains one or two spelling errors. Circle the mistakes and write each word correctly.

I have a pain in my apendix so I have a docter's appointment. ______________ ______________

Salim fractud his wrist attempting to catch a cricket ball. ______________

We thought our cat's swelling addomen meant she was overweight, but it turned out she was pregnent. ______________ ______________

Nowadays children can be imunnised against many diseases. ______________

Why is it that even in hot whether a stethescope feels cold on your chest? ______________ ______________

If you have asthma, the wheeze makes it hard to breath. ______________

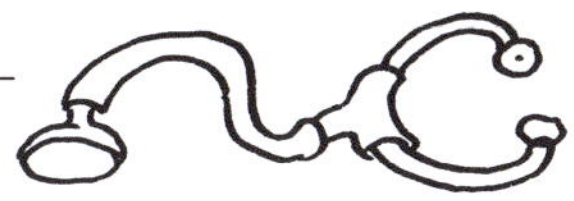

8 Write about a day in your life as a doctor. Use as many list words as you can.

____

____

____

____

Answer: a

Unit 24 Revision

What is sterilis**ation**?

a staring all the time
b the realisation that you do not like stairs
c the process of making something free of germs

1 Write the plural.

symphony ____________
multiple ____________
bacterium ____________
virus ____________
forgery ____________

2 Write the past tense.

explore ____________
magnify ____________
cancel ____________
alter ____________
summarise ____________

3 Add a suffix to each verb to complete the tables.

verb	noun
exclaim	
continue	
define	
satisfy	
repeat	

verb	noun
magnify	
imagine	
vary	
multiply	
explore	

4 Write the list words from Units 19–23 that have silent letters.

____________ ____________ ____________

5 Name these instruments used by a doctor.

____

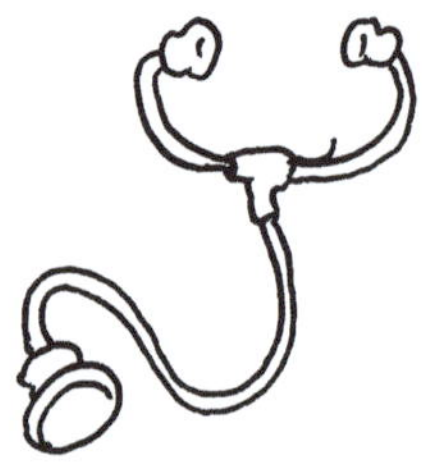

____

6 Write the double letters to complete each word.

va _ _ ination ga _ _ ery monosy _ _ abic a _ _ endix
i _ _ unisation su _ _ ary jewe _ _ ery cance _ _ ation

7 Fill in the missing silent letters.

A _rong move while _res_ling can result in a fractured _rist.
The ex_austed sailors were relieved to arrive in the ca_m waters of the i_land.

8 Add **ary**, **ery** or **ory**.

libr____ groc____ document____ forg____ summ____ explorat____
dormit____ jewell____ second____ gall____ imagin____ laborat____

9 Some letters have gone missing from each sentence. Write each sentence correctly.

At the begning of my project I have t includ a sumry.

____

Kara's favrit game is Monopoly becase she can be an imaginry millonaire.

____

Mr Jaffar is forgtful and somtimes throws his medcines away.

____

I was feeling genrus so I forgave Rita for eating my share of the delicus cake.

____

10 Use the clues to complete the puzzle.

1				A								
2		A		A								
3					A							
4						A						
5		A										
6	A					A						
7									A			
8											A	

1. a musical instrument or body part
2. money for doing work
3. a place to borrow books
4. a train running on a single track
5. a series of loud grating noises
6. a charge made against you
7. a movie that gives information
8. speaking many languages

11 Write a word to complete each riddle.

Q: Why did the boy tiptoe past the medicine cabinet?
A: He didn't want to wake the ________________ tablets.

Q: Why is an optometrist like a teacher?
A: They both examine the ________________.

12 Write the correct form of each word to complete the sentences.

I fell down the stairs the other day and ________________ my ankle.
(fracture)

Roald is great at addition, subtraction and division, but not as good at ________________.
(multiply)

I like music that has ________________ rather than lots of ________________.
(vary) (repeat)

Answer: c

Unit 25

A cygnet is:

a a baby swan
b a tubular fishing net
c an internet expert

Say Listen Look Understand Remember Practise

cyclone ______
cynical ______
cyberspace ______
urgency ______
accuracy ______
literacy ______
numeracy ______
privacy ______
pregnancy ______
diplomacy ______
adequacy ______
delicacy ______
obstinacy ______
buoyancy ______
legacy ______

1 Circle the word in which **cy** has a different sound.

cyclone cynical cyberspace

2 Use letters from each word to make a smaller word in which **c** has a hard sound. Use as many letters as you can.

cyclone	numeracy	obstinacy
______	______	______
pregnancy	legacy	privacy
______	______	______

3 Fill in words ending in **cy**.

The Chinese ______ is the yuan.
The motel's sign read "No ______".
The flood caused ______ evacuations.
A ______ lasts about nine months.

Rule! Most nouns ending in **cy** have base words ending in **nt** or **te**.
infant → infancy delicate → delicacy

4 Write the base word.

accuracy	urgency	obstinacy	buoyancy
______	______	______	______
privacy	adequacy	numeracy	literacy
______	______	______	______

5 What is the base word of **cy**nical? Use a dictionary to find a related word to complete each sentence.

A person who is cynical is called a ______.
A person who is cynical suffers from ______.

Tip! **Cyber** is a word element that shows that the word is related to computers.

6 Write a word beginning with **cyber** to match each definition.

________________ a place where you can eat and use the internet at the same time

________________ the irrational fear of computers or technology

7 Write list words.

Caviar is considered a ________________ in many countries.

Reading and writing are ________________ skills.

Air increases the ________________ of an inflatable object and helps it float.

People who value their ________________ often grow tall hedges.

________________ Tracy caused great devastation in Darwin in 1974.

After practising archery for many months, my ________________ improved.

International ________________ resulted in a peace treaty.

The engineer advised that a new bridge should be built with ________________.

Tip! The prefix **ob** is Greek in origin and can mean either *towards* or *against*.

8 Each word in the puzzle begins with **ob**. Use a dictionary if you need help.

1	O	B									
2	O	B									
3	O	B									
4	O	B									
5	O	B									
6	O	B									
7	O	B									
8	O	B									
9	O	B									
10	O	B									

1. significantly overweight
2. to focus irrational attention on
3. to get or acquire
4. to watch closely
5. unclear or hidden
6. to put an obstacle in the way
7. out of date
8. clearly, evidently
9. an offensive or indecent word or remark
10. antonym of subjectivity

Answer: a

Unit 26

Psittacism is:

a an intelligent joke
b the habit of sitting around all the time
c meaningless, repetitive babble

Say Listen Look Understand Remember Practise

sufficient ____________
territory ____________
appropriate ____________
interrupt ____________
suffocate ____________
graffiti ____________
confetti ____________
colleague ____________
curriculum ____________
suppress ____________
pallor ____________
interrogate ____________
assassin ____________
apparatus ____________
millennium ____________

1 Write each word as prefix + base word. What do you notice about the double letters?

unnecessary ____________	immigration ____________
irregular ____________	dissatisfied ____________
cooperation ____________	surreal ____________

2 Complete the table.

verb	add **ing**
suffocate	
suppress	
interrogate	
suffice	
recommend	
terrorise	

3 Underline the stressed syllable in each word.

territory	committee	graffiti	pallor	colleague
confetti	curriculum	appropriate	suppress	apparatus

4 Sort the list words according to the number of syllables.

2
____
____
____

3
____
____
____
____
____
____
____

4
____
____
____
____
____

Spelling Rules! Book 6 (ISBN 9781420236545) © Helen Pearson, Janelle Ho/Macmillan Education Australia

5 Write a synonym.

coworker ______________

enough ______________

equipment ______________

6 Write one word for each period of time.

10 years ______________

100 years ______________

1000 years ______________

Tip! Nouns ending in **us** or **um** are Latin in origin. The Latin plural forms are still sometimes used.

radius → *radii*   *datum* → *data*

But nowadays most words add **s** or **es** to make the plural.

virus → *viruses*   *vacuum* → *vacuums*

7 Write the plural without adding **s**.

fungus	cactus	curriculum	millennium	crisis
______________	______________	______________	______________	______________

8 Use the correct form of a list word to complete each sentence.

Many animals are ______________ by nature. Once they have established their ______________, they will fight others to protect it.

I am trying to finish my homework but I keep getting ______________.

Dad always insists we are ______________ dressed before we go out.

The hostage was so frightened he had a deathly ______________. Fortunately the ______________ by his captors did not last long.

Our school painted a mural on the fence to prevent ______________.

US President John F Kennedy was ______________ in Dallas in 1963.

The scientific ______________ included beakers, test tubes and Bunsen burners.

Tip! **Collective nouns** can be conventional or creative.

a school of fish   *a wail of weeping willows*

9 Write creative collective nouns for *confetti* and *graffiti*. Then choose two words of your own and write collective nouns for them.

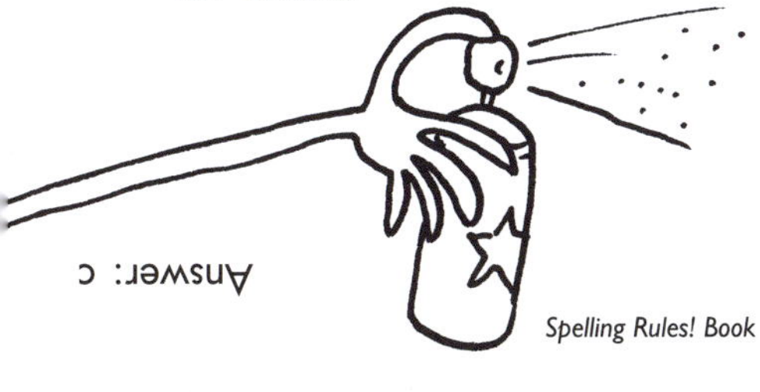

word	collective noun
confetti	
graffiti	

Answer: c

Unit 27

The coccyx is:

a the bone at the base of your spine
b a sick cockatoo
c the nail on your big toe

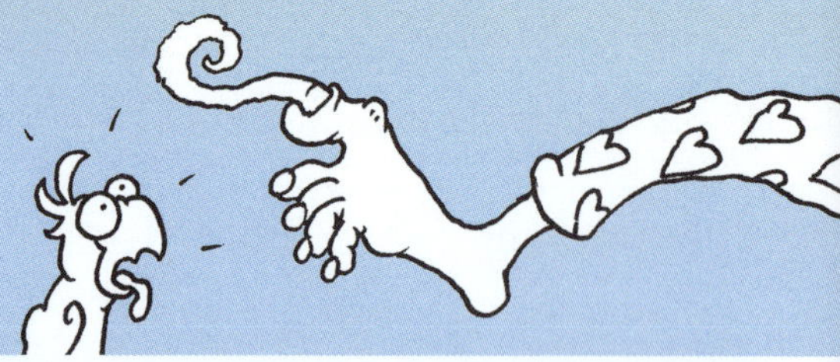

Say Listen Look Understand Remember Practise

successful	____________
eccentric	____________
accentuate	____________
according	____________
accompany	____________
accomplish	____________
accommodation	____________
accumulate	____________
occupation	____________
occurrence	____________
occasionally	____________
piccolo	____________
accolade	____________
desiccate	____________
succulent	____________

Tip! C makes its soft sound when it is followed by **e**, **i** or **y**.

1 Write the list words that have a soft **c** sound. Circle the **c** that makes a soft sound.

____________ ____________

____

2 Write **c**, **cc**, **x** or **xc**.

in__ident	o__upy
o__ygen	e__treme
a__ept	e__ite
e__it	de__eive
de__ide	e__er__ise
a__ident	e__ept
re__eive	a__ess
ne__essary	a__essory
e__use	e__istence

3 Write the base word.

successful	occurrence	occasionally	accommodation
____________	____________	____________	____________

4 Write list words to match the clues.

This is the only word that can take a prefix. ____________

This is a musical instrument. ____________

This word has a drinking vessel in it. ____________

This word has a popular drink in it. ____________

This word has a business or organisation in it. ____________

These words have money in them. ____________ ____________

This word has a thick string in it. ____________

5 Write list words to complete the puzzle. Write your own clue for each word.

Across

1. ______________________________
4. ______________________________
9. ______________________________
10. ______________________________
11. ______________________________

Down

2. ______________________________
3. ______________________________
5. ______________________________
6. ______________________________
7. ______________________________
8. ______________________________
9. ______________________________

6 Proofread this text. The recount has six words that are incorrect. Circle the mistakes. Then write the correct spelling of the words in the boxes.

Acording to Grandpa, the likelihood of an acciddent occuring in our family increases as a birthday approaches. The latest incident happenned just last week. My cousin Susie received a mouth organ as a present. Unfortunately she triped while playing it and hit her head on the computer. She got a black eye, but was lucky she didn't lose a tooth! A jagged crack, however, now runs diagonaly across the computer screen.

Answer: a

Unit 28

A **dis**incen**tive** is:

a a process that removes smells
b a machine that takes away your coins
c something that discourages you from doing something

Say Listen Look Understand Remember Practise

comprehension	______
unchangeable	______
exploration	______
delightful	______
ignorance	______
invisible	______
irrational	______
immobile	______
immovable	______
investigation	______
noticeably	______
symmetrical	______
unintentionally	______
uncritically	______
reversible	______

1 Add a prefix to make the antonym.

legal	mobile	visible
______	______	______
interested	necessary	regular
______	______	______
noticeable	symmetrical	reversible
______	______	______

2 Add a suffix to make a noun.

ignore	press
______	______
exclude	able
______	______
private	selfish
______	______
satisfy	criticise
______	______

Tip! The general term for prefixes and suffixes is **affixes**.

3 Complete the table. The first word in each row is the base word. Add affixes to increase the number of syllables. The first one has been done for you.

1 syllable	2 syllables	3 syllables	4 syllables	5 syllables
		educate	educated	educational
	reverse			
	explore			
	intend			
note				
change				

4 These sentences are too negative. Rewrite each sentence so it makes sense.

My teacher praised me for an unsuccessful entry in the art competition.

____

Everyone looked puzzled as the conclusion to Rex's speech was not quite illogical.

____

The article carefully and uncritically reviewed the evidence.

____

The space in the hall was hard to rearrange as the chairs were not immovable.

____

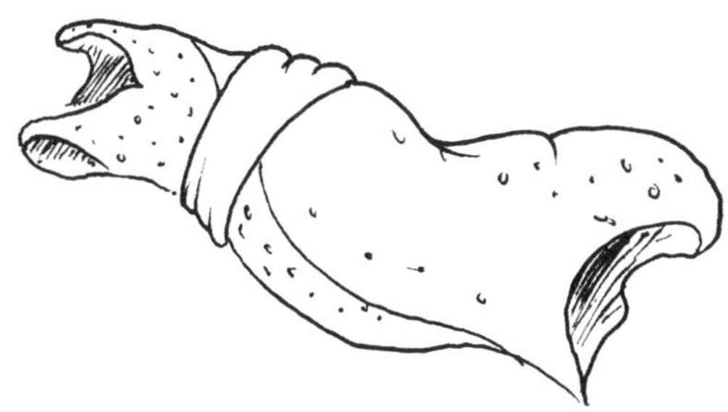

5 Write the correct form of the word to complete each sentence.

Reading ______________ is an important aspect of literacy.
comprehend

Mum bought a ______________ new dress to wear to her birthday ______________.
beauty celebrate

A new family has moved in next door. There are two children and an ______________ puppy.
affection

To ______________ us in our fundraising this year, our teacher showed us a ______________ about the cause we are supporting.
encourage document

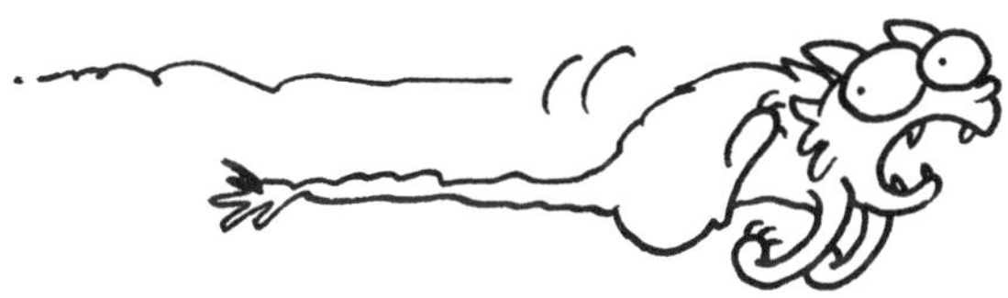

I ______________ trod on our cat's tail this morning.
unintentional

Radio telescopes are an important part of the ______________ of space nowadays.
explore

6 Proofread this text. The text has six words that are incorrect. Circle the mistakes. Then write the correct spelling of the words in the boxes.

I'm writing a detective story. My character, Shirl Lock, is a mischevious girl who loves investigating mysteries. In the begining, her collection of semi-preceous gems goes missing. Her investergation leads her to view her best friend with suspision. In the end, however, her brother is the culprit. To apologise for his misbehaviour, he gives Shirl a beautiful piece of amber to add to her collection. In this story's sequal, the amber itself disappears.

Unit 29

What is a question**naire**?

a a person who asks pesky questions
b someone who doesn't know how much money they have
c a list of questions

Say Listen Look Understand Remember Practise	
currency	__________
exchange	__________
pound	__________
euro	__________
rupiah	__________
baht	__________
allowance	__________
financial	__________
budget	__________
discount	__________
subsidy	__________
purchase	__________
expenditure	__________
millionaire	__________
treasury	__________

1 Write each word as a base word and suffix.

millionaire = __________ + __________
allowance = __________ + __________
financial = __________ + __________
treasury = __________ + __________
accountant = __________ + __________

2 Write the plural.

allowance __________
currency __________
exchange __________
subsidy __________
euro __________

3 Some currencies have a special symbol. Write the currency.

¥ __________ ฿ __________
€ __________ £ __________

4 Write a rhyming word.

pound	euro	baht	millionaire
__________	__________	__________	__________

5 Use each clue to find a smaller word within a list word. Write the small word and the list word.

clue	answer	list word
helps fish steer		
a flower not yet in bloom		
to run after someone		
king of the jungle		
opposite of high		
finish		
a flat circular object		

Spelling Rules! Book 6 (ISBN 9781420236545) © Helen Pearson, Janelle Ho/Macmillan Education Australia

6 Write the correct form of the word to complete the sentence.

Toby was ________________ independent when he was eighteen.
(financial)

The T-shirt her aunt ________________ was too big, so she took it back to the shop to be ________________.
(purchase) (exchange)

Mrs Vazquez says ________________ is important so we know how much money we can spend without getting into debt.
(budget)

The boxes of chocolates were ________________ so Mr Muthu bought ten!
(discount)

Some generous parents are ________________ our excursion to Uluṟu.
(subsidy)

7 These people work with money. Write the occupation to match the definition.

accountant   cashier   teller   money changer

You pay this person at the checkout counter. ________________

You give or receive money from this person in a bank. ________________

This person exchanges one currency for another. ________________

This person keeps track of money in a business. ________________

8 Look at Alex's weekly account and write a report of his budget and expenditure.

Allowance	$20
Savings	$45.60
Magazine	$4.50
Grandma's gift	$7.50
Computer game	$6.95
Pool entry	$3.00
Ice-cream	$2.70
	$24.65

____

____

____

____

____

____

Answer: c

Spelling Rules! Book 6 (ISBN 9781420236545) © Helen Pearson, Janelle Ho/Macmillan Education Australia

Unit 30 Revision

To rappel is to:

a rap without a sense of rhythm
b descend a steep slope using a rope
c turn magnets away from each other

1 These words need single or double consonants added. Write the words correctly using the consonants in brackets.

mi___e___ium (l, n)	va___i___ation (c, n)	a___o___odation (c, m)
a___a___in (s, s)	gra___i___i (f, t)	de___i___ate (s, c)
cu___i___u___um (r, c, l)	mi___io___aire (l, n)	o___a___iona___y (c, s, l)

2 Write the plural.

territory	committee	piccolo	confetti	currency
______	______	______	______	______

3 Most of the vowels have been left out of these sentences. Write each sentence correctly.

My sstr s xtrmly obstnt so w cn rrly prsd hr t chng hr mnd.

____

____

Prsnlly, I thnk m ncl is a lttl ccntrc bcs h njys rdng th dctnry.

____

____

I m rsrchng th dffrnc n byncy f bjcts in frsh wtr nd slt wtr.

____

____

4 Write the correct form of the words to complete each sentence. You will need to add either one or two affixes.

Diana tried ______ (success) to thread a needle and felt ______ (frustrate) when she pricked her finger yet again.

Faizal is an ______ (accomplish) ______ (violin). So far, his greatest ______ (achieve) has been ______ (perform) at the Town Hall.

Uncle Max is a ______ (sympathy) and ______ (friend) kind of person. He's quite shy and ______ (rare) says much. However, when he has a story to tell, we give him our full ______ (attend) because his stories are always very ______ (humour).

5 Write a word to match each definition. Each word has the letters **cy**, but not as a suffix.

hurricane ______________

two-wheeled transportation ______________

a conical, evergreen tree ______________

use again ______________

book of knowledge ______________

a poison ______________

6 Write a synonym and an antonym.

	synonym	**antonym**
buy	______________	______________
new	______________	______________
rational	______________	______________
sufficient	______________	______________

7 Write the correct form of the word to complete each sentence.

I closed my door to get some ______________.
private

Please check your work for ______________.
accurate

Snails are considered a ______________ in France.
delicate

Objects have greater ______________ in salt water than in fresh water.
buoyant

8 Add **c**, **cc**, **x** or **xc**.

o__upation	su__essful	e__ercise	de__ide
e__entric	re__eive	e__tra	a__entuate
e__cite	a__complish	e__ept	e__act

9 Write as many words as you can by adding affixes to the base word. Choose one member of the word family to use in your own sentence.

able: ____

____

believe: ____

____

excite: ____

____

Answer: b

Unit 31

A fascicle is:

a an interesting fact
b a broken icicle
c a small bundle

Say Listen Look Understand Remember Practise

ascend ______
descend ______
transcend ______
obscene ______
adolescent ______
fluorescent ______
iridescent ______
effervescent ______
miscellaneous ______
susceptible ______
convalesce ______
scintillate ______
conscience ______
conscientious ______
resuscitate ______

1 Each word has a soft **c** sound. Use some of the letters in each word to make a word with a hard **c** sound.

obscene	miscellaneous
______	______
susceptible	resuscitate
______	______

2 Write the list word that contains the smaller word.

dole	ran
______	______
ride	lane
______	______
it	science
______	______
scene	ale
______	______

Tip! *Ascend*, *descend* and *transcend* all have the same Latin origin, *scandere*, meaning *to climb*. The prefix *a* or *ad* means *towards*, *de* means *away from* and *trans* means *beyond*.

3 Write what each word means. Use a dictionary to check your answer.

descend = ______
ascend = ______
transcend = ______

4 Use a word containing **sce** or **sci** and alliteration to invent a product name.

Erin's effervescent energy drink

______

______

Spelling Rules! Book 6 (ISBN 9781420236545) © Helen Pearson, Janelle Ho/Macmillan Education Australia

5 These sets of words are sometimes confused. Write the correct word to complete each sentence.

ascent accent assent

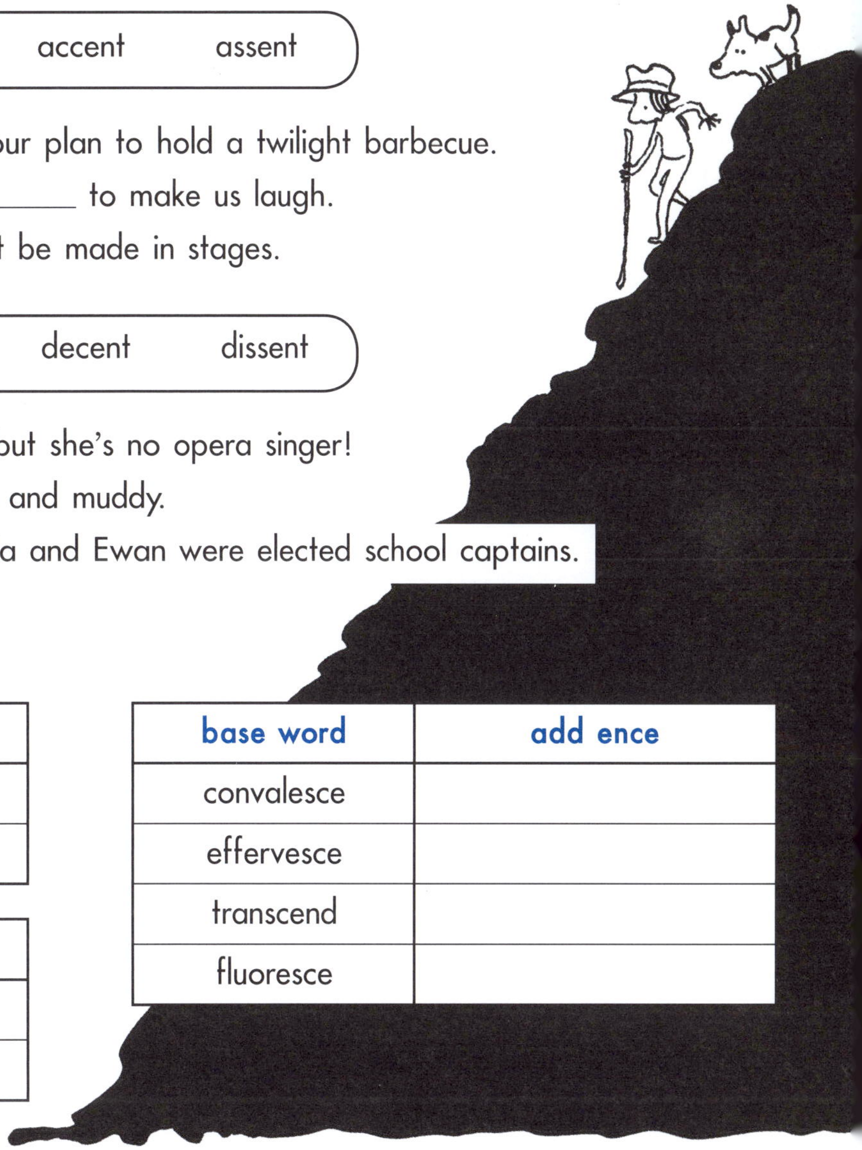

The principal gave his ________________ to our plan to hold a twilight barbecue.
Don told the joke with a French ________________ to make us laugh.
The ________________ of Mount Everest must be made in stages.

descent decent dissent

She's got a ________________ singing voice but she's no opera singer!
Be careful, as the ________________ is steep and muddy.
There was no ________________ when Magda and Ewan were elected school captains.

6 Add the suffix to make the noun.

base word	add ion
fascinate	
resuscitate	

base word	add ity
susceptible	
obscene	

base word	add ence
convalesce	
effervesce	
transcend	
fluoresce	

7 Write the correct form of a list word to complete each sentence.

Grandma is ________________ well after her operation, although she is still ________________ to infection.

The dance troupe put on a ________________ performance at the concert. They wore ________________ costumes that appeared to glow in the spotlights.

Dad contributed many ________________ objects to our school's garage sale – but he bought even more junk home again!

8 Write the list words that have meanings related to light. Use a dictionary if you need help.

____

Choose one of these words and use it in a sentence.

____

Answer: c

Unit 32

Syzygy is:

a a country near Kazakhstan
b the conjunction or opposition of two heavenly bodies
c the noise sausages make when you throw them on a barbecue

Say Listen Look Understand Remember Practise

skiing ____________
queued ____________
asphalt ____________
amateur ____________
havoc ____________
awkward ____________
anemone ____________
rhyme ____________
rhythm ____________
sleuth ____________
nuisance ____________
naively ____________
eclipse ____________
impromptu ____________
labyrinth ____________

1 Sort the list words according to the number of syllables. Underline the stressed syllable in each word.

1 ____________ ____________ ____________

2 ____________ ____________ ____________ ____________ ____________ ____________ ____________

3 ____________ ____________ ____________ ____________

4 ____________

2 Break the word into its base word and suffix.

skiing = ________ + ________
queued = ________ + ________
naively = ________ + ________

3 Write list words.

The new puppy caused ____________ when it got into the groceries.
They discovered the pungent smell was caused by new ____________ being put down on the road.

An ____________ of the sun is an amazing natural event.
Rada is going ____________ for the first time this winter.

Tip! **Mnemonics** are tricks to help you remember something more easily.
*Eclipse – it **clips** from **e** to **e**.* *With as**th**ma, each brea**th** is hard.*

4 Choose three list words you find difficult, then make up a mnemonic for each.

5 Write a list word so that the first and last part of each sentence rhymes.

The intrepid ________________ found the thief in a booth.
The poet gave up crime to search for the perfect ________________.
The crowd had a festive mood, as we waited and patiently ________________.
The locusts caused ________________ as they ate through the paddock.
We planned a simple barbecue; the party was quite ________________.

6 Use **nuisance** as an adjective and a noun.

adjective: ____

noun: ____

7 Circle the word that doesn't make sense in each sentence. Write the correct word in the box.

The anomalies in the rock pool waved their tentacles.	
We queried for an hour to enter the stadium.	
Keep quiet and don't be such a nuance!	
This competition is only open to armatures.	

8 Find one word or phrase in each sentence for which a list word is a synonym. Circle the word or phrase you have chosen and write the synonym in the box.

The basement was a maze of storerooms and passageways.	
Dad gave an off-the-cuff speech at his birthday dinner.	
Sasha offered to assist at the carnival even though the timing was inconvenient for her.	

> Tip!
> **Similes** describe something by comparing it to something else using *like* or *as*.
> *Her hair was like silk.*
> **Metaphors** describe something by saying it *is* something else.
> *Her hair was black silk.*

9 Write a simile and a metaphor using the word *rhythm*.

simile: ____

metaphor: ____

Answer: b

Unit 33

An **angklong** is:
a a very long rowboat
b an Indonesian musical instrument
c an angle on the long side of a rectangle

Say Listen Look Understand Remember Practise

trek	____
snorkel	____
mammoth	____
deluxe	____
carnival	____
rampage	____
maestro	____
berserk	____
gruesome	____
cologne	____
abseil	____
souvenir	____
gourmet	____
silhouette	____
entrepreneur	____

1 Fill in the silent letters.

gourme_ sil_ouette colo_ne

Tip! Some words can be both nouns and verbs.
I ***spy*** *a fly.* *I didn't know he was a* ***spy****.*

2 Write a sentence for each meaning of these words.

trek (noun): ____

trek (verb): ____

snorkel (noun): ____

snorkel (verb): ____

3 Use a dictionary to find out where each list word comes from.

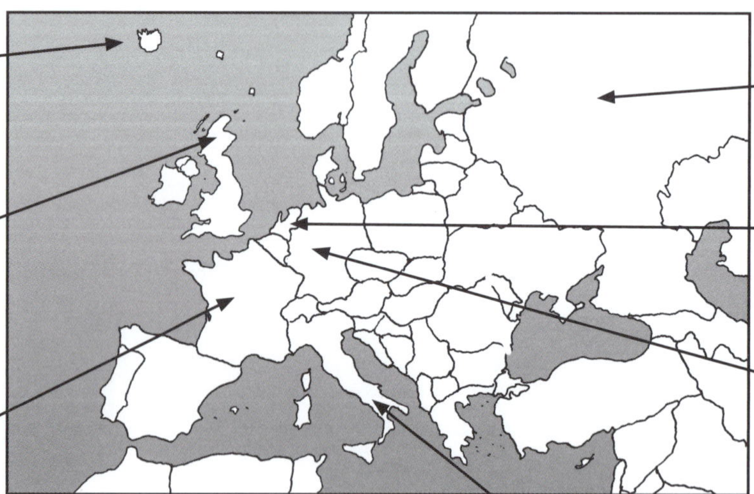

Spelling Rules! Book 6 (ISBN 9781420236545) © Helen Pearson, Janelle Ho/Macmillan Education Australia

4 Use list words to complete the puzzle.

Across

2. wild and frenzied
5. perfume
6. long and difficult journey
7. tube for breathing underwater
8. of excellent taste
10. gigantic
11. business person
12. a holiday keepsake
13. destructive behaviour
14. of superior quality

Down

1. to descend using a rope
3. an outline
4. a distinguished musician
8. horrific
9. a travelling fair or sports meet

5 Write list words you might use when talking about these topics.

war ____________________

sports ____________________

people ____________________

your senses ____________________

Answer: b

Unit 34

An **astro**labe was a medieval instrument used to measure:

a the altitude of the stars and planets
b how much water stars hold
c how many labradors there are in space

Say Listen Look Understand Remember Practise

asteroid	
astronaut	
astronomy	
comet	
galaxy	
meteor	
shuttle	
dimension	
futuristic	
chronology	
medieval	
terrestrial	
archaeologist	
palaeontology	
Renaissance	

1 Sort the list words according to whether they are related to time or space. Some words may fit both categories.

time: ____________________

space: ____________________

Write the word that is French in origin and means "rebirth".

____

Tip! The prefix *astro* comes from the Greek word for *star*.

2 Use the definitions to complete the puzzle.

1	A	S	T	E	R					
2	A	S	T	E	R					
3	A	S	T	R	O					
4	A	S	T	R	O					
5	A	S	T	R	O					

1. a structure that revolves around the sun
2. name of the symbol *
3. a space traveller
4. the study of the universe
5. a person who studies the universe

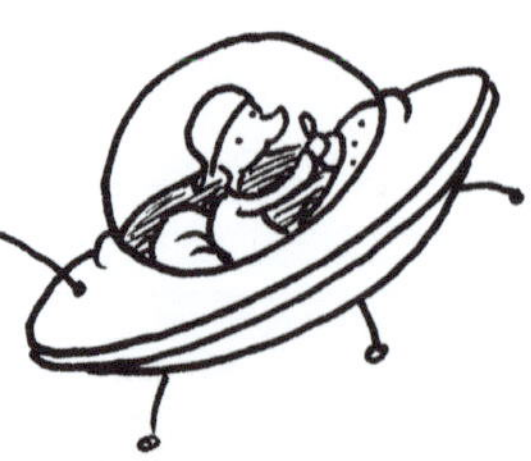

3 Use each clue to find a smaller word within a list word. Write the small word and the list word.

clue	answer	list word
a small dwelling		
opposite of go		
male adults		
to have a break		

Tip! An **idiom** is a group of words always used in a fixed expression.

4 Write the meaning of each idiom.

out of this world ________________________________

to work like clockwork ________________________________

par for the course ________________________________

a dog's breakfast ________________________________

in the nick of time ________________________________

know it like the back of your hand ________________________________

5 Write the correct form of a list word to complete each sentence.

Two of the first ________________ to land on the moon were Neil Armstrong and John Glenn.

Takei has had a ________________ rise in the company. He's worked there for only a year and is already a manager.

A ________________ is someone who studies fossils in order to discover more about extinct plants and animals. Part of the job is working out the ________________ order of events so as to trace the evolution of these plants and animals.

A shape like a circle or square is two-________________ because it only has length and breadth. A sphere and a cylinder have three ________________ because they also have depth and can contain things.

Aliens can also be called ________________ creatures. Most movies portray such creatures as frightening.

Answer: a

Unit 35 Revision

One of the longest words in the English language is **floccinaucinihilipilification**. It means:

a having hallucinations about sheep
b climbing hills repeatedly
c the act of estimating something as worthless

1 Write the word for each picture.

 ____________

 ____________

 ____________

 ____________

 ____________

 ____________

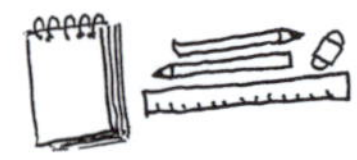 ____________

 ____________

2 Complete the table by building word families.

verb	past tense	noun	adjective	adverb
wonder				
	exploded			
		desperation		
			suspicious	
				decisively

3 Some of the vowels have been left out of these words. Add the missing vowels.

____wkw____rd　　t____tion
____rch____logist　　____rie
fl____rescent　　baz____r
s____ven____r　　f____na

4 Some of the consonants have been left out of these words. Add the missing consonants.

ex____e____　　fra____ure
enviro____ent　　bu____et
____eumonia　　co____oa
e____erve____ence　　a____lete

5 Write a word to match each definition.

a long piece of music played by a large orchestra ____________
someone new and inexperienced ____________
able to speak many languages ____________
all the words a person knows ____________
to enlarge a sound or image ____________
a false name ____________
a many-sided shape ____________

6 Each word has been written as it sounds. Rewrite it correctly.

converless	daybew	show fur	orkustrah
________	________	________	________
rithum	canserlation	missalayneeus	backteeriah
________	________	________	________

7 Add **g** or **j**.

ad_acent	avera_e	passen_er	_ustice	ur_ent
re_oice	fra_ile	challen_e	pre_udice	_ud_ement

8 Add the letters that make the **er** sound.

p___manent	v___tual	c___cular	t___minate	dist___b
j___ney	p___l	reh___se	c___tesy	s___ch

9 Add **al**, **el** or **le**.

practic__	seri__	chort__	sequenti__	vehic__
gradu__	parall__	optic__	partic__	skelet__

10 Circle any words in each sentence that do not make sense. Rewrite each sentence so it makes sense.

The train terminals at the next stop.

___

Our team was unsuccessful because we trained hard and played well.

___

At weddings I love throwing graffiti at the bride and groom.

___

When I had affluence the doctor listened to my chest with a periscope.

___

"You'd better have a good exclamation for being late," said Boris.

___

At dinner, Doug ate an access of dessert. No wonder his digression was affected!

___

Answer: c

Spelling Rules! Book 6 (ISBN 9781420236545) © Helen Pearson, Janelle Ho/Macmillan Education Australia

List words in unit order

Unit 1
average
advantage
passenger
urgent
fragile
revenge
challenge
pledge
justice
rejoice
junction
prejudice
adjacent
adjustment
judgement

Unit 2
rejection
detection
exhibition
exhaustion
digestion
distinction
admission
permission
submission
extension
suspension
expansion
evolution
resolution
revolution

Unit 3
desperation
cooperation
appreciation
devastation
association
deception
prescription
explosion
decision
erosion
invasion
exclusion
collision
persuasion
provision

Unit 4
flee
pursue
statue
venue
cocoa
mosquito
rodeo
eerie
simile
guarantee
refugee
committee
verandah
debut
alibi

Unit 5
government
parliament
cabinet
politician
minister
senator
representatives
governor
premier
opposition
president
election
democracy
monarchy
federal

Unit 7
permanent
terminate
persevere
mineral
several
mirth
virtual
memory
temporary
curse
surplus
disturbance
yearn
adjourn
sojourn

Unit 8
electrician
employee
employer
manager
lawyer
pioneer
engineer
translator
sculptor
surgeon
scientist
pharmacist
chef
athlete
chauffeur

Unit 9
ability
stability
durability
probability
acceptability
predictability
respectability
changeability
availability
irritability
possibility
visibility
flexibility
responsibility
accessibility

Unit 10
accent
ascent
device
devise
cemetery
symmetry
stationery
stationary
bizarre
bazaar
affect
breath
excess
descent
wander

Unit 11
environment
rainforest
pollution
greenhouse
climate
recycle
ozone
ecology
irrigation
conservation
deforestation
flora
fauna
sustainable
atmosphere

Unit 13
opinion
tuition
rational
occasional
prior
senior
superior
inferior
exterior
posterior
median
alliance
radiant
peculiar
diarrhoea

Unit 14
optical
practical
skeletal
serial
gradual
beneficial
sequential
especially
essentially
excel
rebel
parallel
particle
chortle
vehicle

Unit 15
wondrous
disastrous
humorous
hazardous
miraculous
indigenous
mysterious
suspicious
envious
rebellious
ferocious
voracious
precarious
advantageous
spontaneous

Unit 16
novel
novelty
novice
innovate
innovation
vocal
vocabulary
advocate
vociferous
invoke
provoke
notice
notify
annotate
reminisce

Unit 17
solution
toxic
method
experiment
acid
alkaline
temperature
evaporate
thermometer
theory
equipment
chemical
microscope
hypothesis
laboratory

Unit 19
satisfaction
definition
repetition
conversation
alteration
continuation
declaration
cancellation
explanation
exclamation
variation
multiplication
application
identification
notification

Unit 20
library
salary
imaginary
secondary
summary
documentary
gallery
grocery
jewellery
forgery
category
exploratory
accusatory
dormitory
laundry

Unit 21
monopoly
monolith
monotonous
monosyllabic
multiple
multipurpose
multimedia
multicultural
multilingual
polygon
polyphonic
omnivore
omnipresent
omnipotent
omniscient

Unit 22
symphony
phonetic
microphone
cacophony
synonym
antonym
pseudonym
anonymous
sympathy
empathy
telepathy
majesty
majority
magnify
magnificent

Unit 23
medicine
bacteria
virus
pregnant
fracture
organ
influenza
abdomen
intestine
capsule
appendix
vaccination
immunisation
pneumonia
stethoscope

Unit 25
cyclone
cynical
cyberspace
urgency
accuracy
literacy
numeracy
privacy
pregnancy
diplomacy
adequacy
delicacy
obstinacy
buoyancy
legacy

Unit 26
sufficient
territory
appropriate
interrupt
suffocate
graffiti
confetti
colleague
curriculum
suppress
pallor
interrogate
assassin
apparatus
millennium

Unit 27
successful
eccentric
accentuate
according
accompany
accomplish
accommodation
accumulate
occupation
occurrence
occasionally
piccolo
accolade
desiccate
succulent

Unit 28
comprehension
unchangeable
exploration
delightful
ignorance
invisible
irrational
immobile
immovable
investigation
noticeably
symmetrical
unintentionally
uncritically
reversible

Unit 29
currency
exchange
pound
euro
rupiah
baht
allowance
financial
budget
discount
subsidy
purchase
expenditure
millionaire
treasury

Unit 31
ascend
descend
transcend
obscene
adolescent
fluorescent
iridescent
effervescent
miscellaneous
susceptible
convalesce
scintillate
conscience
conscientious
resuscitate

Unit 32
skiing
queued
asphalt
amateur
havoc
awkward
anemone
rhyme
rhythm
sleuth
nuisance
naively
eclipse
impromptu
labyrinth

Unit 33
trek
snorkel
mammoth
deluxe
carnival
rampage
maestro
berserk
gruesome
cologne
abseil
souvenir
gourmet
silhouette
entrepreneur

Unit 34
asteroid
astronaut
astronomy
comet
galaxy
meteor
shuttle
dimension
futuristic
chronology
medieval
terrestrial
archaeologist
palaeontology
Renaissance

List words in alphabetical order

abdomen	Unit 23
ability	Unit 9
abseil	Unit 33
accent	Unit 10
accentuate	Unit 27
acceptability	Unit 9
accessibility	Unit 9
accolade	Unit 27
accommodation	Unit 27
accompany	Unit 27
accomplish	Unit 27
according	Unit 27
accumulate	Unit 27
accuracy	Unit 25
accusatory	Unit 20
acid	Unit 17
adequacy	Unit 25
adjacent	Unit 1
adjustment	Unit 1
admission	Unit 2
adolescent	Unit 31
advantage	Unit 1
advantageous	Unit 15
advocate	Unit 16
affect	Unit 10
alibi	Unit 4
alkaline	Unit 17
alliance	Unit 13
allowance	Unit 29
alteration	Unit 19
amateur	Unit 32
anemone	Unit 32
annotate	Unit 16
anonymous	Unit 22
antonym	Unit 22
apparatus	Unit 26
appendix	Unit 23
application	Unit 19
appreciation	Unit 3
appropriate	Unit 26
archaeologist	Unit 34
ascend	Unit 31
ascent	Unit 10
asphalt	Unit 32
assassin	Unit 26
association	Unit 3
asteroid	Unit 34
astronaut	Unit 34
astronomy	Unit 34
athlete	Unit 8
atmosphere	Unit 11
availability	Unit 9
average	Unit 1
awkward	Unit 32
bacteria	Unit 23
baht	Unit 29
bazaar	Unit 10
beneficial	Unit 14
berserk	Unit 33
bizarre	Unit 10
breath	Unit 10
budget	Unit 29
buoyancy	Unit 25
cabinet	Unit 5
cacophony	Unit 22
cancellation	Unit 19
capsule	Unit 23
carnival	Unit 33
category	Unit 20
cemetery	Unit 10
challenge	Unit 1
changeability	Unit 9
chauffeur	Unit 8
chef	Unit 8
chemical	Unit 17
chortle	Unit 14
chronology	Unit 34
climate	Unit 11
cocoa	Unit 4
colleague	Unit 26
collision	Unit 3
cologne	Unit 33
comet	Unit 34
committee	Unit 4
comprehension	Unit 28
confetti	Unit 26
conscience	Unit 31
conscientious	Unit 31
conservation	Unit 11
continuation	Unit 19
convalesce	Unit 31
conversation	Unit 19
cooperation	Unit 3
currency	Unit 29
curriculum	Unit 26
curse	Unit 7
cyberspace	Unit 25
cyclone	Unit 25
cynical	Unit 25
debut	Unit 4
deception	Unit 3
decision	Unit 3
declaration	Unit 19
definition	Unit 19
deforestation	Unit 11
delicacy	Unit 25
delightful	Unit 28
deluxe	Unit 33
democracy	Unit 5
descend	Unit 31
descent	Unit 10
desiccate	Unit 27
desperation	Unit 3
detection	Unit 2
devastation	Unit 3
device	Unit 10
devise	Unit 10
diarrhoea	Unit 13
digestion	Unit 2
dimension	Unit 34
diplomacy	Unit 25
disastrous	Unit 15
discount	Unit 29
distinction	Unit 2
disturbance	Unit 7
documentary	Unit 20
dormitory	Unit 20
durability	Unit 9
eccentric	Unit 27
eclipse	Unit 32
ecology	Unit 11
eerie	Unit 4
effervescent	Unit 31
election	Unit 5
electrician	Unit 8
empathy	Unit 22
employee	Unit 8
employer	Unit 8
engineer	Unit 8
entrepreneur	Unit 33
envious	Unit 15
environment	Unit 11
equipment	Unit 17
erosion	Unit 1
especially	Unit 14
essentially	Unit 14
euro	Unit 29
evaporate	Unit 17
evolution	Unit 2
excel	Unit 14
excess	Unit 10
exchange	Unit 29
exclamation	Unit 19
exclusion	Unit 3
exhaustion	Unit 2
exhibition	Unit 2
expansion	Unit 2
expenditure	Unit 29
experiment	Unit 17
explanation	Unit 19
exploration	Unit 28
exploratory	Unit 20
explosion	Unit 3
extension	Unit 2
exterior	Unit 13
fauna	Unit 11
federal	Unit 5
ferocious	Unit 15
financial	Unit 29
flee	Unit 4
flexibility	Unit 9
flora	Unit 11
fluorescent	Unit 31
forgery	Unit 20
fracture	Unit 23
fragile	Unit 1
futuristic	Unit 34
galaxy	Unit 34
gallery	Unit 20
gourmet	Unit 33
government	Unit 5
governor	Unit 5
gradual	Unit 14
graffiti	Unit 26
greenhouse	Unit 11
grocery	Unit 20
gruesome	Unit 33
guarantee	Unit 4
havoc	Unit 32
hazardous	Unit 15
humorous	Unit 15
hypothesis	Unit 17
identification	Unit 19
ignorance	Unit 28
imaginary	Unit 20
immobile	Unit 28
immovable	Unit 28
immunisation	Unit 23
impromptu	Unit 32
indigenous	Unit 15
inferior	Unit 13
influenza	Unit 23
innovate	Unit 16
innovation	Unit 16
interrogate	Unit 26
interrupt	Unit 26
intestine	Unit 23
invasion	Unit 3
investigation	Unit 28
invisible	Unit 28
invoke	Unit 16
iridescent	Unit 31
irrational	Unit 28
irrigation	Unit 11
irritability	Unit 9
jewellery	Unit 20
judgement	Unit 1
junction	Unit 1
justice	Unit 1
laboratory	Unit 17
labyrinth	Unit 32
laundry	Unit 20
lawyer	Unit 8
legacy	Unit 25

SPELLING RULES AND TIPS

Adding **ion**

If a verb ends in **ibe**, drop the **e** and change the **b** to **pt** before adding **ion**.

describe → *description*

If a verb ends in **eive**, drop the silent **e** and change **iv** to **pt** before adding **ion**.

receive → *reception*

If a word ends in **t**, change **t** to **ss** before adding **ion**.

admit → *admission*

If a word ends in **nd**, change **d** to **s** before adding **ion**.

extend → *extension*

If a word ends in **lve**, change **ve** to **ut** before adding **ion**.

solve → *solution*

If a word ends in **y**, change the **y** to **i** and add **cation**.

multiply → *multiplication*

Some exceptions: *vary* → *variation* *satisfy* → *satisfaction*

Adding **al**

If a noun ends in **ce**, change the **ce** to **ti** before adding **al** to make the adjective.

confidence → *confidential*

Exceptions: *office* → *official* *practice* → *practical*

Adding **ity**

Words ending in **ible** and **able** are adjectives.

These words may also add **ity** as a second suffix.

Adding **ity** changes the adjective to a noun.

probable → *probability* *visible* → *visibility*

Homographs

A word that is spelt the same as another but has a different meaning is called a **homograph**.

bear = a big furry mammal

bear = to endure or to carry

novel = a book of fiction

novel = new

Spelling Rules! Book 6 (ISBN 9781420236545) © Helen Pearson, Janelle Ho/Macmillan Education Australia